AF543006

Soil Colloids and Ion Exchange

NIPA® GENX ELECTRONIC RESOURCES & SOLUTIONS P. LTD.
New Delhi-110 034

About the Author

Dr. Anandkumar Naorem, currently employed as a scientist at ICAR-Central Arid Zone Research Institute in Jodhpur, India, previously held the position of Head-in-charge at ICAR-CAZRI, RRS-Bhuj, India. He completed his bachelor's degree at Assam Agricultural University, Assam, India, and pursued his master's degree in soil microbiology and bioformulation at the College of Post-Graduate Studies, Central Agricultural University, Meghalaya, India. His doctoral research, conducted at Bidhan Chandra Krishi Viswavidyalaya in West Bengal, India, focused on the remediation of soil heavy metals for safer crop cultivation.

Dr. Naorem, who has authored several national and international publications, has received national recognition, including the 2015 Best Zonal Master's Thesis award from the Indian Society of Soil Science and the UGC-Maulana Azad National Fellowship for Minority Students (India). He is acknowledged for his contributions as a young scientist by numerous societies and organizations, having led various research projects on soil quality in arid regions, studies on elevated carbon dioxide levels, and investigations into halophytes. Notably, he has played a key role in international initiatives promoting spineless cactus as a dryland feed option in Gujarat.

---

for other volumes of
The Professional's Notes Series

The Professional's Notes Series
Volume 05
Soil Colloids and Ion Exchange

Anandkumar Naorem
Scientist, Division of IFS
ICAR-Central Arid Zone Research Institute
Ministry of A&Fw, Government of India
Jodhpur-342003, Rajasthan, India

NIPA® GENX ELECTRONIC RESOURCES & SOLUTIONS P. LTD.
New Delhi-110 034

NIPA® GENX ELECTRONIC
RESOURCES & SOLUTIONS P. LTD.

101,103, Vikas Surya Plaza, CU Block
L.S.C.Market, Pitam Pura, New Delhi-110 034
Ph : +91 11 27341616, 27341717, 27341718
E-mail: newindiapublishingagency@gmail.com
www: www.nipabooks.com

For customer assistance, please contact
Phone: + 91-11-27 34 17 17
Fax: + 91-11- 27 34 16 16
E-Mail: feedbacks@nipabooks.com

© 2025, Authors

Print ISBN: 978-93-58875-47-8

ebook ISBN: 978-93-58876-21-5

All rights reserved. No part of this publication may be reproduced, stored in a retrieval system or transmitted in any form or by any means, including electronic, mechanical, photocopying recording or otherwise without the prior written permission of the publisher or the copyright holder.

This book contains information obtained from authentic and highly reliable sources. Reasonable efforts have been made to publish reliable data and information, but the author/s, editor/s and publisher cannot assume responsibility for the validity, accuracy or completeness of all materials or information published herein or the consequences of their use. The work is published with the understanding that the publisher and author/s are not attempting to render any professional services. The author/s, editor/s and publisher have attempted to trace and acknowledge the copyright holders of all material reproduced in this publication and apologize to copyright holders if permission and/or acknowledgements to publish in this form have not been taken. If any copyrighted material has not been acknowledged, please write to us and let us know so that we may rectify the error, in subsequent reprints.

Trademark Notice: NIPA®, the NIPA® logos and their presentations (the way they are written/presented) in this book are the trademarks of the publisher and hence may not be used without written permission, if copied or used without authorization, the infringer will be prosecuted as per law.

NIPA® also publishes books in a variety of electronic formats. Some content that appears in print may not be available in electronic books, and vice versa.

Composed and Designed by NIPA®.

Preface

Welcome to Volume 05, dedicated to "Soil Colloids and Ion Exchange." In this volume, we embark on a fascinating journey into the intricate world of soil colloids and their role in ion exchange processes. Soil colloids, often referred to as the "heart" of the soil, are minute particles that play a crucial role in soil fertility, nutrient retention, and environmental sustainability. In this volume, we dive into the properties and behavior of soil colloids, exploring their interactions with ions, water, and organic matter, and their implications for soil health and ecosystem function. Ion exchange, a fundamental process mediated by soil colloids, regulates the availability and mobility of nutrients in the soil, influencing plant growth, microbial activity, and overall soil fertility. By understanding the mechanisms of ion exchange, we gain insights into the dynamic relationships between soil chemistry, biology, and physics, and their impact on soil nutrient dynamics and ecosystem resilience.

Furthermore, soil colloids serve as reservoirs for organic matter, pollutants, and trace elements, affecting soil quality, environmental contamination, and human health. By examining the fate and transport of contaminants in soil colloids, we can develop strategies to mitigate pollution, remediate contaminated sites, and promote environmental sustainability. Studying soil colloids and ion exchange processes is essential for addressing pressing environmental challenges, such as soil degradation, nutrient depletion, and pollution. By unraveling the mysteries of soil colloids, we can develop innovative solutions to enhance soil fertility, conserve natural resources, and promote sustainable agriculture for future generations.

With gratitude and anticipation,

Anandkumar Naorem

Contents

SOIL COLLOIDS AND ION EXCHANGE IN SOIL.

- a colloidal system - heterogeneous mixture (disperse in state of fine subdivision)
  - atleast 2 phases → dispersed phase → dispersion medium. (continuous medium)
- size limits 1 µm — 1 nm | 1 µm = 10^{-6} mm = 10^{-3} m | 1 nm = 10^{-12} mm = 10^{-9} m.
- If solid (dispersed phase) + water (↳ dispersion medium) ⟶ 'sol.'
- (< 1 nm) uni-phase solⁿ —— sol —— suspensions (> 1 µm)
  (particle size) 1 nm - 1 µm.
- most important properties — large intersurfacial area — charge density
- soil colloidal fraction crucial for — ion-exchange
  - nutrient availability & fixation
  - soil physical properties — structure — HC — infiltration
  - soil management

↓ divided on the basis of
- nature of linkages present
- types of compound formed

Inorganic (covers)
- aluminosilicate layer-lattice clay minerals (temperate regions)
- hydrous oxides and hydroxides of Fe, Al, Si, Mn in clay size dimension (tropical & sub-tropical)
- amorphous silicate
  ↳ without a clearly defined shape.

Organic.
- soil humus (temperate)

hydrous oxides = oxides + H_2O
Hydroxides = OH containing

INORGANIC SOIL COLLOIDS

- chief colloidal fraction in inorganic nature is aluminosilicate layer lattice clays.
  ↳ derived from the silicate minerals.
  ↓ most commom minerals in earth's crust - 90% of.
- dominated by silicates occuring as primary minerals (inherited from Ig. & Meta. rocks)
- and as secondary minerals (from weathering of ↑)
- SiO_4^{4-} tetrahedron (basic structural unit of silicates)

- depending on the arrangement of SiO_4^{4-} tetrahedron.
  ↳ silicates are classified into: diff. groups.

- BASICS OF PHYLLOSILICATE MINERALS.

- Early 1920s - clays are mostly crystalline

STRUCTURAL UNITS IN PHYLLO.

↳ closest packing of spheres
(- to maintain stability)

↓

packing of anions around a central cation
↳ one ionic spheres touches 6 neigh. spheres.
↳ called as hexagonal closest packing.

↓

creates two voids

void A	void B.
- central cation in it have 4 surrounding spheres.	- central cat. have 6 surr. spheres.
- cation in tetrahedral site is said to be in 4-fold or tetrahedral coordination state	- 6-fold or octahedral site
- bonded to 4 oxide ions (O^{2-})	- 6 hydroxyl/oxide ions.

SiO_4^{4-} EXPLAINED

(at no.)
Si → 14 electrons 2 8 4 → needs 4.
O → 8 electrons 2 6 → needs 2.

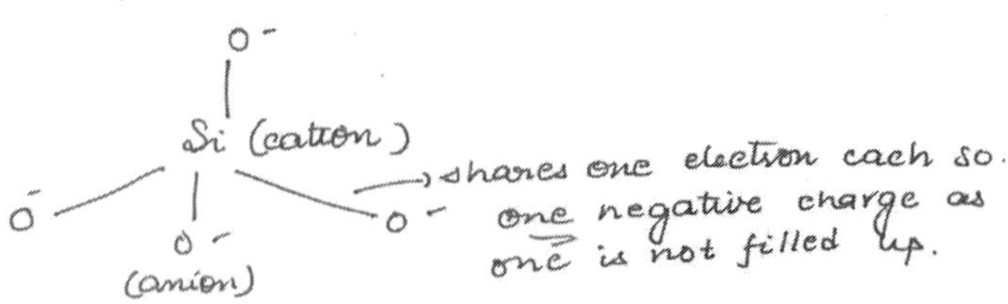

= SiO_4^{4-}

Al → 13 (2, 8, 3) → needs 5 electrons
Mg → 12. (2, 8, 2) → needs 6 electrons.

- SiO_4^{4-}, $Al(OH)_6^{3-}$

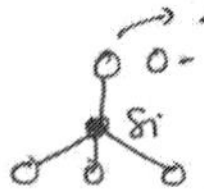

→ free apical O^{2-} ions (ready to form bond with other polyhedral atoms)

- 2 ways of filling the octahedral sites with a central cation
- Al^{3+} or Mg^{2+}

REDUCING THE NET NEGATIVE CHARGE PER UNIT Mg-OCTAHEDRON.

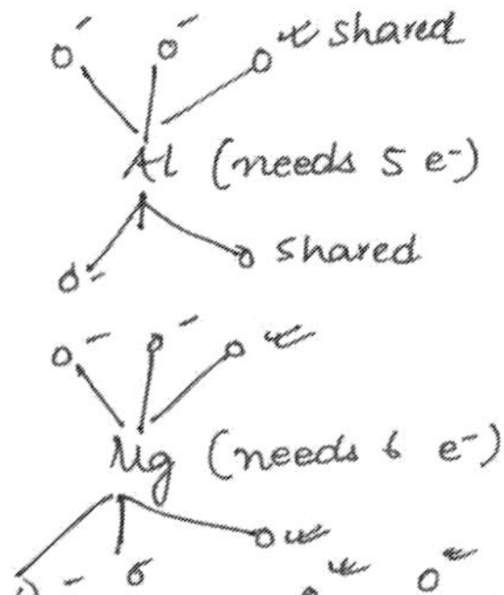

= $Al(OH)_6^{3-}$

= $Mg(OH)_6^{4-}$

= The network = $Mg_3(OH)_6$.

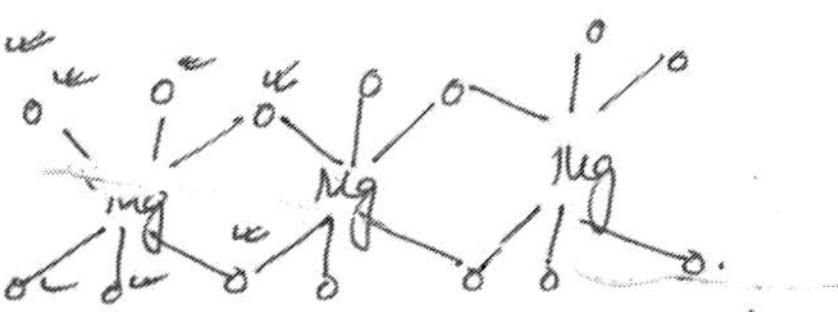

Mg shares 1/3rd of uni-negative charge ~~per unit Mg-octa.~~ of each of the 6 octahedral hydroxyl ions.

- each hydroxyl ion - shared by 3 Mg^{2+} ions.
- known as trioctahedral sheet = occupied by a divalent cation
- " " dioctahedral sheet = " " " trivalent

The network $Al_2(OH)_6$.

GOLDSCHMIDT'S LAWS

- shape and size of the crystal structure governed by
- ratio of number of units
- " " ionic sizes.
- properties of polarization of its structural units
- Allowance → repulsive forces in ionic compounds especially when a central cation is small eg. Li^+ and the surrounding anions have virtual contact with one another.

GOLDSCHMIDT'S LAWS I AND II

(I) — In an ionic crystalline compound
- isomorphous replacement of one cation by another
- without incurring any change in order of crystal pattern
- permitted — provided radii of the cation replaced and substituted agree — 10–15%

→ isomorphous substitutions ⟶ may lead to charge imbalance

substitution of Si^{4+} by Al^{3+}/or
" " ~~Mg~~ Al^{3+} by Fe^{2+}/Mg^{2+} ⟶ excess negative charge.

↓

Balanced by
- ~~app~~ simultaneous substitution
- retention of oppositely charged ions

(II) RADIUS RATIO LAW

- When the no. of anions around a central cation
- satisfy the charge ... completely.
- no. of anions – determined by ratio of ionic radii of the cation to the anions. (O^{2-} reference as anion)

Ionic radii (nm)

O^{2-}	0.140	0.lord
Si^{4+}	0.039.	0.dimiq
Al^{3+}	0.051	0.dsl
Mg^{2+}	0.066.	0.dobb
Fe^{3+}	0.064.	0.dober

Co-ordination number of 12 not found in ionic crystals?

- Max^{m} radius ratio — 0.732-1 which corresponds to co-ord. no. of 8 → not possible greater than 8.

$r = 0.414R$

$r = 0.225R$

- Conclusion

Radius of tetrahedral site = 0.035 nm O. dimis

" " octahedral site = 0.050 nm. O. dosed

i) — radius upto 0.41 (O. role) times that of oxide ion — can be accomodated in tetrahedral site

- radius upto 0.73 times . . . .
O. time octahedral site

ii) Si^{4+} ion can remain in 4-fold co-ordir state in tetr. shee;
Al^{3+} . . . . . . 4 & 6 . . . . . . tetrah & octa.

iii) Fe^{3+}, Fe^{2+}, Mg^{2+} can be accom. in octahedral sh sites.

iv) K^{+} can be acc. in dodecahedral arrangement of oxide ions i.e in between 2 hexagonal arrays of oxide ions.

- Common phyllosilicate — 1:1 and 2:1 type.

ORGANIC SOIL COLLOIDS

- Humic colloids
- 70-80% of OM consists of humic substances — humic ā, fulvic ā, humin.

continuous decomposition & encompassing alteration of proteins, carbohy. fats, resins, wax and etc

f.6 synthesis of complex humic substances.

- dark, partly aromatic, amorphous
→ characterised by flexible polyelectrolyte behaviour, polyfunctional groups and high mol. wt.

eg. polycations / polyanions / POLYELECTROLYTE → polymers whose repeating units bears an electrolyte group.

aromatic = stable hydrocarbon
eg. benzene ring

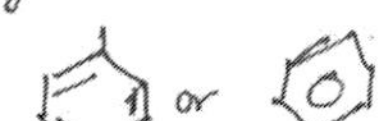
alternate double bong

- CEC 200-250 cmol (p^+) kg^{-1} of soil.
- functional groups
  - carboxylic (-COOH)
  - phenolic (⌬-OH)
  - hydroxyl (-OH)
  - amide
  - amine

  } That's why proton donors or proton acceptors depending on pH
- also impregnate (fill) in soil mineral matter (forming clay humic complexes)

SOURCES OF CHARGES

ISOMORPHOUS SUBSTITUTION (pH INDEPENDENT)

- different charges but similar ionic radii
- giving rise to imbalance of charge
- creates negative charge when high valency ions subs. by low valency.

  eg. Si^{4+} by Al^{3+} in tetrahedral sheet in mica, vermiculite, illite

  Al^{3+} by Mg^{2+} / Fe^{2+} in octahedral sheet in montmorillonite.

- creates positive charge.

  forming $Mg_2AlO(OH)_2^+$ in trioctahedral sheet

- It leads to pH-independent charges (constant) in vermiculites and chlorites

pH DEPENDENT CHARGE

- kaolinite
- aluminosilicate clay
- hydrous oxides and hydroxides of Fe, Mn, Al, Si
- allophane
- amorphous colloids
- organic colloids

- negative charge develops due to the dissociation of proton
  - from exposed hydroxyl group
  - bound H_2O of constitution at edge and surface.

- p^H dependent
- carboxylic, phenolic groups act as weak acids. (phenolic → at p^H 9.0)
  - carboxylic ↓ ionizes at lower p^H (5.5-6.0)
  - depending upon dissociation constant of the medium and nature of surrounding medium.
- Substituted of phenolic group by like nitrophenols are stronger acids.
  - ↓ due to electron withdrawing character of nitro group
  - ↓ ionizes at intermediate p^H 6.0-9.
  - Dissociation constant of acid (Ka): quantitative measure to know the strength of an acid.

- +ve charge haven't reported - organic
- But, organic sp. bonded to $-NH_2$ group may protonate at low p^H → yield +ve charged $R-NH_3^+$.
- exposed edge/surface hydroxyl group can act as acid and base (amphoteric)

↓

depending upon the preponderance of H^+/OH^- ions in vicinity

↓

which also warrants there must be an intermediate p^H when the surface is uncharged

↓

ZPC (Zero Point of charge) – p^H at which net surface charge is 0.

↳ colloids (which are mixtures of permanent and depen. charge)

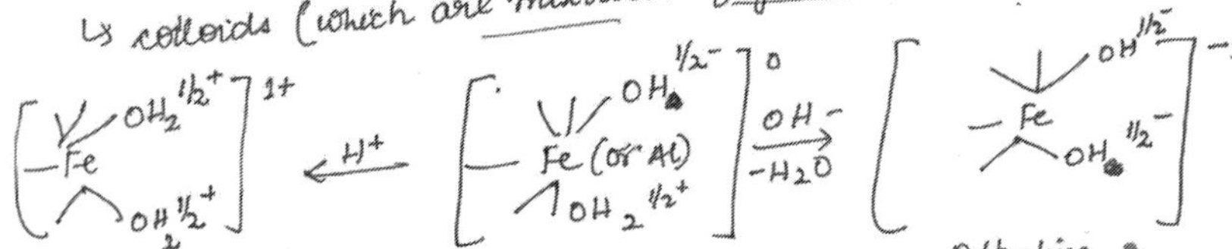

Acidic (p^H < ZPC) towards +ve charge and anion exchange

Neutral (at the p^H of ZPC)

Alkaline (p^H ≥ ZPC) towards -ve charge and cation exchange

ZPC
- silicic acid – 2.0 pH
- ~~gibbsite~~ geoshite (α- $Fe^{III}OOH$) – 8.5
- gibbsite [$Al(OH)_3$] – 9.

- Modification of ~~surface~~/edge charge chara.
  ↓
  change of ZPC.

- Phosphate fixation by ligand exchange.
(exchange of neutral OH_2- ligand to Fe or Al by applied $H_2PO_4^-$ ion) → raises the surrounding –ve charge and pushes the ZPC to lower pH

~~lower pH~~ ↑ higher ZPC ↓ ~~higher~~ pH lower	ZPC ↓ lower pH	↑ –ve charge surrounding. ZPC ↑

ie stronger H^+ ion concn is reqd. in soil soln to render ZPC

–ve charge → ↑ higher pH
↓

LIGAND
ion or molecule that binds to a central metal atom to form a co-ordination complex

- Intense weathering ~~increases~~ shifts ZPC towards higher pH. owing to accumulation of Ox. & hy. of Fe & Al.
- ZPC of Ultisol/Oxisol > Inceptisol
- OM also shifts ZPC towards lower pH

–ve charge
↓
lower pH

In kaolinite

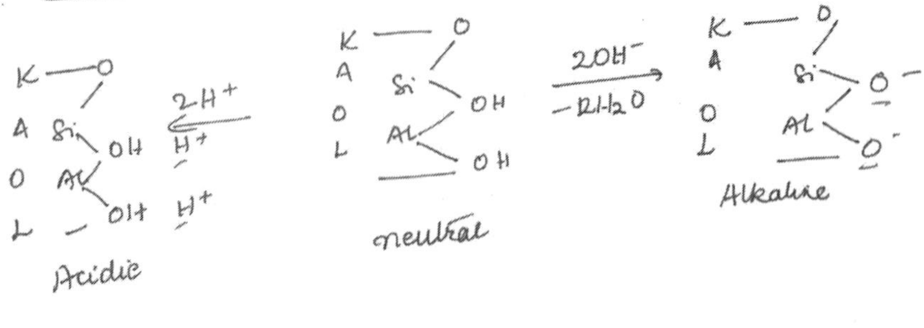

-ve charge

pH independent (permanent)
- within layer-lattice of the clay minerals

pH-dependent
- exposed surface/edge of clay minerals
- soil OM
- hydrous oxides and hydroxides of Fe and Al.

ELECTRICAL DOUBLE LAYER OF SOIL COLLOIDS

- net charge of the colloid is balanced by counter ions.
- electrostatically attracted by the soil colloids (opp. charge)
  have a tendency to move into the bulk soil
  two opposite forces results in a distribution of counter ions such that their concn decreases as distance increases from the surface.
  forms two regions
  - more or less fixed layer at uni-molecular or uni-ionic distance (Helmholtz layer)
  - more diffuse (due to thermal or kinetic movement) → Gouy-Chapman layer.

electrostatically = slow moving or constant charges without acceleration

- Bulk soln (more uniform of the charges)
- Excess cation and less anion in double diffuse layer as compared to the bulk solution.
- known as Stern model

STABILITY OF SOIL COLLOIDS

- soil colloids -ve charged
- cations in diffuse layer
  } → creates electrostatic potential from
  Ⓟ → soil colloid surface
  Ⓡ → Bulk soil soln
- In such a way
  sharp change in Helmholtz layer (PQ)
  more gradual change in Gouy-Chap. (QR)
- The potential difference between fixed part (Q) and freely mobile portion (R) – Zeta Potential (ξ)

- determines the stability
- also known as electrokinetic potential. DIFFUSION
- More this ξ → more distance → more repulsion → more buoyancy → less coalesce → more dispersed.
- If the layers considered as parallel plate electrical condenser carrying charge e per cm², and d apart, ξ will be

$$\xi = \frac{4\pi e d}{D}$$

D → Dielectric constant of the medium (H_2O)
↓
ability of a substance to store electrical energy in an electric field.

use this for Helmholtz layer

- COAGULATION
- On addition of electrolyte into soil soln.

electrolytes = minerals that carry electric charge.

electrolyte contains both anions and cations

- cations accumulate in soln side in vicinity of PC.
- Upon gradual addition, neutralization of charge on surface through ion-pair formation.

ION PAIR FORMATION

anion and cation come together

solvated pair, solvent shared, contact

↳ increase in cationic charge due to higher bonding energy of cation for the surface.

↳ lower e and d

↳ electrostatic attraction ↓

↳ double layer compressed → concomitant (naturally occurring) redn in buoyancy → due to gravity → settling → coagulate/flocculate

✓ When ξ attains value of 0 → isoelectric state

✓ ZPC = Isoelectric state when there is no specific absorption

→

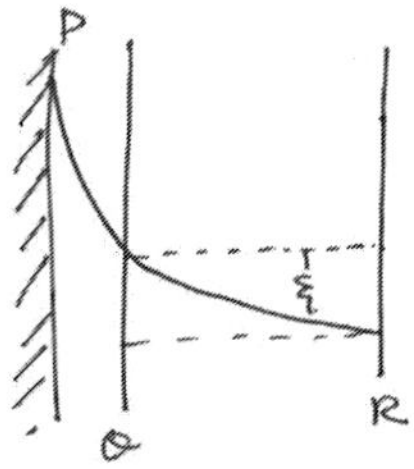

✓ ξ - function of two charges < pH indep / dependent.

- difference between ZPC and iso. point
- But in pH-dependent charges -- .. like hydrous oxides and hyd. of Fe and Al or SOM → a polypeptide mol. (amphoteric)

in its isoelectric state regarded as a neutral molecule even though ions occur in equally distribut.

ELECTROMETRIC (ELECTROCHEMICAL) PROPERTIES OF SOIL COLLOIDS

- advantageous when soil colloids regarded homoionic to a single cation.

eg. acid clay can be produced by passing / leaching of the clay with 0.1 N HCl repeatedly → f. b electrodialysis to remove excess electrolytes

→ using H^+ ion-exchange resins (pass the clay suspension through it).

ION-EXCHANGE RESIN

Insoluble matrix (0.5-1 mm diam) beads, usually white/yellow, fabricated from an organic polymer.

- porous, high surface area
  - trapping of ions

ELECTROPHORESIS

- solid part are moved using an electric field.

ELECTRO-OSMOSIS

- liquid part are moved.

support solid material is gel

gel, membrane, capillary etc.

ELECTROKINETIC PHENOMENA IN SOIL COLLOIDS.

i) — two glass tubes filled with water
— encasing two platinum electrodes into moist clay
- connected to an external (EMF) → to give electric current

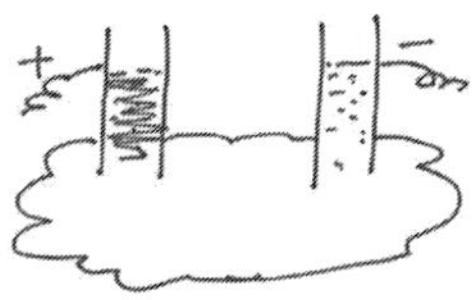

→ The positive terminal becomes turbid → clay move under electric field towards positive electrode
→ known as electrophoresis. | -ve charged particles free to move.

ii)

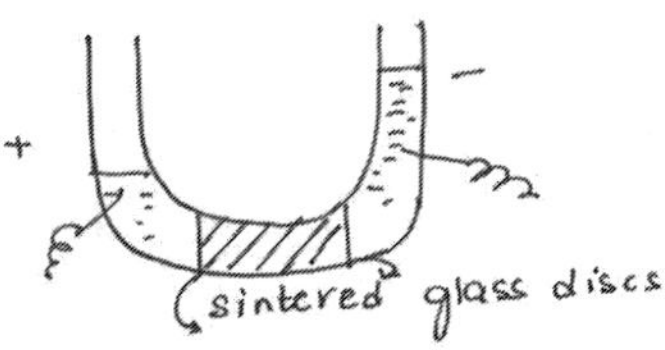

- U-tube
- clay plug at centre with sintered glass discs.
- apply electric field
- -ve terminal rises water until difference in two arms becomes constant
- known as electro-osmosis. | -ve charge particles restricted to move.

iii) Closer examination of Electro osmosis.
- expecting a pressure difference to induce electric current
- But is due to the application of electric field.
- The ensuing current → streaming current
→ corresponding potential difference → streaming potential

$$\left(\frac{\text{velocity of electro-osmotic flow of } H_2O}{\text{applied electric field}}\right)_{\text{Pressure difference}=0}$$

↓ =

Taking separately ↕

$$\left(\frac{\text{streaming current}}{\text{Pressure difference}}\right)_{\text{applied electric field}=0}$$

i.e. $\left[\frac{v}{X}\right]_{\Delta P=0} = \left[\frac{i}{\Delta P}\right]_{X=0}$

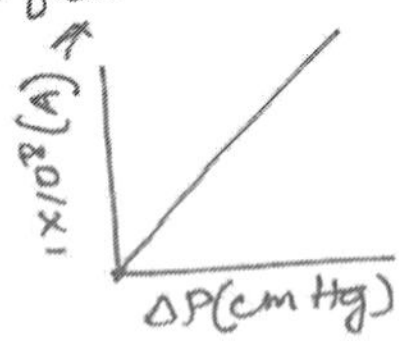

↓ electro-osmotic mobility

↳ streaming current density generated per unit pressure difference.

- Those quantities are characteristics of the electrical double layer at colloidal / ~~sur~~ solution interface.

iv) 1878, Dorn → lagsag

colloidal particles under sedimentation in H_2O lead to the develop. of EMF at different depths when two electrodes at diff depths are inserted

- opposite of electrophoresis
- sedimentation potential
- Dorn effect.

VISIBLE AND INFRARED SPECTROSCOPIC STUDIES OF HUMIC COLLO

(Basic Principles)

PLANCK EQUATION

= particle nature of light

laqdood

1900, German Max Planck

↓

proposed Blackbody radiation

(visible glow that solid objects radiate when heated)

- intensity of this radiation varies with wavelength of the light

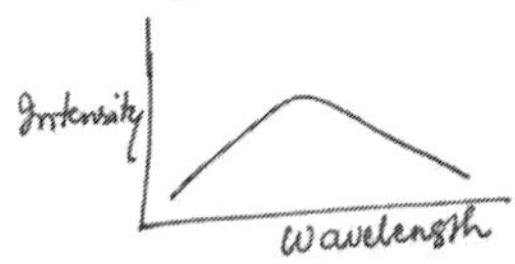

it ~~decreases~~ increases with decrease in wavelength

reaches maxm and then decreases.

But in electromagnetic wave theory,

intensity ~~increases to a~~ keep on a increasing.

→ energy radiated is not continuous

so called. quantized. ← discrete amounts (quantum)

→ amt of energy E associated with a quantum of radiant energy depends on the frequency of the radiation.

$E = h\nu$ → frequency

$= \frac{hc}{\lambda}$ → velo. of light

λ → wavelength

Planck's constant (6.626×10^{-34} J.s) ← b.bnb X10-34

$= \underline{6.626 \times 10^{-34}}$ kg. m²/s.

1 J = 1 kg. m²/s²

Light → composed of stream of small particles called PHOTONS

↓

Each photon carries one quantum of energy.

b.bnb X10-34

b.bnb.

Electronic transitions

moving of electron from one energy state to higher energy level which can be used to determine the structure of the molecule

atomic orbital: mathematical function ~~of that~~ describes the wave like behaviour of either one or a pair of e⁻ in an atom

s p d f

Sigma bond (σ - bond)

strongest ~~bond~~ covalent bond. formed by head on overlapping between atomic orbitals. (direct overlapping of orbitals).

π - bond (Pi-bond)

weaker than σ-bond (partial overlapping of atomic orbitals)

- electronic transitions in humic molecules

↓ lead

spectral absorption bands in UV and visible region (200–800 nm)

The electrons involved are those in

a) σ-bond

b) π-bond

c) non-bonding e⁻

anti-bonding orbitals' → molecular orbitals that if occupied by electrons, weakens the bond between two atoms and helps to raise the energy of the molecule.

The energy radiated is given by Planck's Equation

$$E = h\nu$$
$$= h\frac{c}{\lambda}.$$

- absorption of light energy in UV and vis. Region by humic colloids — accompanied by promotions of e⁻ from ground state to higher energy

$\sigma \rightarrow \sigma^*$
$\pi \rightarrow \pi^*$
$n \rightarrow \sigma^*$
$n \rightarrow \pi^*$

} anti bonding orbitals.

$\sigma^* \rightarrow$ much higher energy level.

→ compounds having more π-bonds will absorb more energy at longer wavelength..

$E\downarrow \rightarrow \lambda\uparrow$

→ extensive conjugation (C–C bonds and C= bonds alternately) further reduce the energy.

→ true in aromatic compounds.

→ delocalization of π-e⁻ takes place as the energy level decreases → pushing the absorption band far in the visible region.

The absorption spectrum is given by:-

Lambert-Beer's Law

$A = \log \frac{I_0}{I} = abc$.

I_0 — intensity of incident

I — transmitted light.

a = molar extinction coefficient of the light absorbing sub. (ie humic colloids)

b = path length

c = concentration.

- However, as compared to UV region and visible, higher no. of peaks → infrared region

wavelength 2.5 – 15 µm

0.8 to 2.5 (near IR)

15 to 200 µm. (Far IR.)

- In IR region, absorption shown as a function of wave no.
  ↳ reciprocal of wavelength
  ie 12,500 – 4000 cm⁻¹.

- energy of absorption in IR is smaller than UV and visible because of longer wavelength.

$E = h\nu$
$= h\frac{c}{\lambda}$

- associated with vibrations of molecule
  ↳ stretching (distance between bond changes but not position) — symmetric / asymetric
  ↳ Bending (position changes)
  - In-plane
  - out-of plane.

Finger-Print region of IR

- region that contains a very complicated series of absorptions (1500 – 500 cm⁻¹)
- mainly due to all manners of bending vibrations within the molecule
- can used to identify compounds.

HYDROCARBONS

ALIPHATIC	AROMATIC
- Straight chain	- ring with conjugated system of bonds
- related compounds called allyl	- aryl
- single, double, triple bond (alkanes, alkenes, alkynes) can exist anywhere	- should form a conjugate system ie alternate single and multiple bond.
- have localized e-	- delocalized e-

↳ ABSORPTION OF ENERGY IN THE VISIBLE REGION.

- absorption of radiant energy in visible region by humic and fulvic acids indicates degree of → aromatization and
→ relative preponderance of aromatic and aliphatic nature of a colloid.
→ comparative absorption at 465 nm λ (aliphatic group), 665 nm λ (aromatic group)
- Higher degree of aromatization → higher absorption at longer wavelengths.
→ Fulvic colloids (lower polymer) → has high E_4/E_6.
→ E_4/E_6 → better index indicating preponderance.
→ Fulvic colloids → more aliphatic structures.

↳ ABSORPTION OF ENERGY IN INFRARED REGION

→ The composition of functional groups in humic colloids can be known from their IR spectrum.
→ Presence of phenolic (-OH), amide, methyl, free-NH — carboxylic, carbonyl and others → from fingerprint region.
→ degree of aromatization → can be found out from the presence of absorption peaks/bands in 1500 – 1600 cm^{-1} wave no.

COILING IN THE HUMIC SUBSTANCES : HYDROPHOBIC BOND

- Humic colloids — both → hydrophilic (almost all f.g) / hydrophobic (C-H group)
  - → in aqueous medium remain in coiled state.
- Such coiling is more in humic colloids than fulvic coll.
  - ↓ more polycondensate nature.
- → interaction between hydrophobic backbone and H_2O is energetically / thermodynamically unfavourable.
- → That's why water molecules are drawn together by surface tension and non-polar groups tend to aggregate
  - ↓ coiling
  - → minimize contact of their contact area with H_2O.
- → called hydrophobic bond → but a misnomer (not an appropriate name)
  - ↳ results under thermodynamic compulsion.

RHEOLOGICAL PROPERTIES OF SOIL CLAYS

- Rheology → science of flow of fluids, deformation process, developing with time.
- → flow behaviour of clay suspension largely depend on mode and nature of interaction between the clay particles.
  - Three types.
    - EF (Edge - face) } responsible for card - house structure
    - EE (edge - edge) } throughout clay suspension
    - EF (face - face) → Vander Waal's force.
      - → causes thickening of clay particles
- at edge → +ve charged double layer } as a result EF attraction.
- at face → -ve . . . .
  - (internal mutual flocculation)
  - ↙ causing high viscosity (high resistance to flow).

- FF linkage — reduce EF linkage → ↓ viscosity

→ When electrolytes are added

↓

both the edge and face double layers are compressed

↳ at this time,
nature of viscosity is determined by two factors: —

a) balance between EF linkage and FF repulsion.

b) enhanced Vander Waal's FF and EE attractions.

→ Montmorillonite shows sensitivity (change in viscosity) in addition of electrolyte.

↳ possible way to identify presence of mt as dominating clay suspension.

→ Illite and kaolinite → less sensitive

Reason:-

In this viscosity buffer curves, shows a distinct peak/hump.

- due to nature of its clay lattice to expand in polar liquids → which causes easy accomodation of hydrated cation → upto 70-80% Base sat.

↓

high value of volume fraction (ϕ)

Acc. to Einstein equation.

vis. coefficient of clay suspe. ← $\frac{\eta}{\eta_0} = 1 + 2.5\,\phi$. for ↳ spherical suspended parti.

η_0 ↓ water.

(at same temp)

- So, mixtures of mont with non-exp. → reduce η → ↓ ϕ.

ION-EXCHANGE IN SOIL

- exchange → equivalent amount of ions → phases in equilibrium → reversible.
- cation exchange – 1850 Thomson f.b Thomas Way

    ↙

    Leach soil with ~~$(NH_4)_2SO_4$~~ $NH_4(SO_4)_2$

    ↓ upon filtration

    less NH_3 was recovered instead Ca, Mg, K were detected

    ↙

    called as base exchange before but replaced as H^+ also involved in cation exchange.

- composition of soil solution changes due to
    - ↳ dilution (rain or irrigation)
    - ↳ ion uptake by plants
    - ↳ leaching
    - ↳ fert. application
    - ↳ use of brackish ground H_2O for irrigation
    - ↳ reclammation of salt-affected soils.
    - ↳ sewage and sludge farming

↳ CATION EXCHANGE CAPACITY. → $CEC = S \times \sigma$ — surf. charge density; S — specific surface; $\sigma = \frac{\sqrt{2\varepsilon nkT}}{\pi \sinh(z e \psi_0 / 2kT)}$

- exchange or interchange capacity of the soil to adsorb and exchange cations.
- sum of exchangeable cations that can be absorbed by a soil colloidal surface
- SI unit :- cmol(p^+) kg^{-1} (p — proton)   AEC : cmol (e^-) kg^{-1}
- CGS :- meq per 100 g

BONDING ENERGY OF EXCHANGEABLE CATIONS

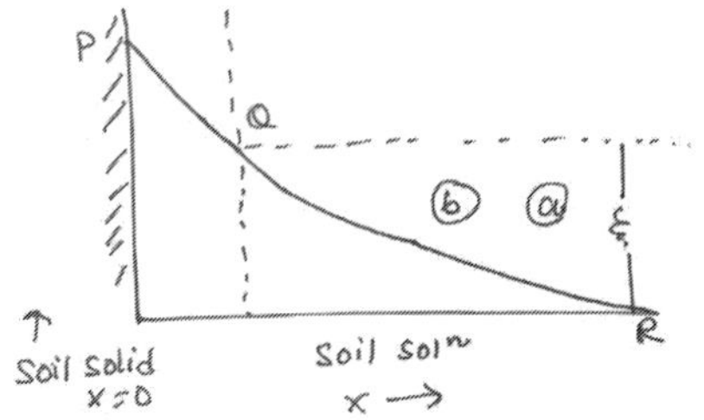

- Ionic strength of the solution (measure of electric field) (I)

$$I = \frac{1}{2}\sum m_i z_i^2$$

where m_i = molality

$= \frac{\text{no. of moles of solute}}{\text{mass of solvent in kg}}$

i = solution phase

z = valency of the ion.

Σ = summation to cover all ionic species in 'i'

- activity (a) = effective concentration

$$a_i = \gamma_i m_i$$

↳ activity coefficient.

At infinite dilution $\gamma_i \to 1$, $a_i \to m_i$

- γ_i → by Debye-Hückel Extended Law (solution that contain ionic solutes don't behave ideally even at low concn).

Peter Debye
Erich Huckel

$$-\log\gamma_i = \frac{A z_i^2\sqrt{I}}{1 + B d\sqrt{I}}$$

A and B = constants

d = diameter of the hydrated cation.

Anand Naorem

Nitrogen undergoes a number of transformations that involve organic, inorganic and volatile compounds. These transformations occur simultaneously and may be viewed in terms of a cycle called N-cycle in which the element is shuttled back and forth at the discretion of microflora. The different components of N transformations are as follows:

a) Microbial mineralization of N
b) Microbial immobilization of N
c) ~~Denitri~~ Microbially mediated loss of N through denitrification
d) N-fixation.

Minerализation of N

The microbial conversion of ~~organi~~ organically bound N to the more mobile inorganic state is known as mineralization of N. As a consequence of mineralization, ammonium and nitrate are generated. These products delineates two distinct microbiological processes —

i) Ammonification : Transformation of Organic N to NH_4^+ ion,

ii) Nitrification : Transformation (oxidation) of NH_4^+ ion to nitrate (NO_3^-) ion.

Almost all of the N found in surface soil horizons, is in organic combination within the compounds like the total humus N is in this form)

i) amino acids (20-50% of the total humus N is in this form)
ii) Amino-sugar (5-10%)
iii) Nucleic acids (< 1%)

The rate at which organic nitrogen is converted to ammonium and nitrate is termed as ~~mineralized~~ mineralization rate.

Net change in the amount of inorganic nitrogen (ΔN_i) = Organic nitrogen mineralized − (N assimilated by the microflora + N uptake by plants + Leaching of N + denitrification of N).

The nitrogenous compounds present in the soil organic fraction persist for long periods in nature. It might be due to the fact that nitrogenous compounds form complexes or polymers rendering the nitrogen-containing substances less susceptible to microbial attack.

In unamended soil, Organic C and Organic N are mineralized at parallel rates and the ratio of CO_2-C to N_i produced is essentially constant at approximately 7 to 15 : 1. Protein-poor residues favour CO_2 evolution whereas protein-rich materials favour N_i (inorganic N) release.

The immediate source of the NH_4^+ ion formed by ammonification is water soluble N fraction of the organic residues. Therefore, the rapidity of the ammonium release from crop residues is often closely related to its quantity of water-soluble N.

PROTEIN DECOMPOSITION

Microorganisms synthesize extracellular proteolytic enzymes for the decomposition of proteins. The proteolytic enzymes, called proteases, cleave the protein molecule to polypeptide, simple peptides and finally to the free amino acids that are the end products of protease action. The reaction is a hydrolysis as the enzyme ruptures the peptide bond ($-\overset{O}{\overset{\|}{C}}-\overset{H}{\overset{|}{N}}-$) by the addition of water.

Proteolytic organisms may be bacteria (eg. Pseudomonas, Bacillus, Clostridium, Serratia and Micrococcus), fungi (eg., Alternaria, Aspergillus, Mucor, Rhizopus etc) and actinomycetes.

~~Bacteria dominate~~ in neutral or alkaline environment
Fungi frequently release less NH_4^+ ion than bacteria since the fungi assimilate more of the N for the purpose of cell synthesis.

The amino acids liberated serve as C and N sources for innumerable heterotrophs, each of which may be able to utilize one or several of these compounds. The N of the amino acids is removed as NH_3 prior to significant decomposition of the C-containing portion of the molecule.

$$R{-}CH_2{-}\underset{NH_2}{\overset{H}{C}}{-}COOH \xrightarrow{\text{Deamination}} R{-}CH{=}CH{-}COOH + NH_3$$

$$R{-}\underset{NH_2}{\overset{H}{C}}{-}COOH + \tfrac{1}{2}O_2 \xrightarrow[\text{deamination}]{\text{Oxidative}} R{-}\underset{O}{\overset{}{\underset{\|}{C}}}{-}COOH + NH_3$$

$$R{-}\underset{NH_2}{\overset{H}{C}}{-}COOH + 2H \xrightarrow[\text{deamination}]{\text{Reductive}} RCH_2{-}COOH + NH_3$$

$$R{-}\underset{NH_2}{\overset{H}{C}}{-}COOH \xrightarrow{\text{Decarboxylation}} RCH_2 \cdot NH_2 + CO_2$$

NUCLEIC ACID METABOLISM

They are second only to proteins in importance as nitrogenous substrates for the microflora. Plants and animal tissues and microbial cells contain two types of nucleic acids ribonucleic acid (RNA) and deoxyribonucleic acid (DNA). Structurally, each is a polynucleotide, that is, a polymer of the structural unit known as mononucleotide.

The microbial decomposition is mediated by the enzymes ribonuclease and deoxyribonuclease that act on RNA and DNA, respectively, or by enzymes that hydrolyze both RNA and DNA. The latter are termed nucleases.

Extracellular ribonuclease is formed by the species of :
Bacteria → Bacillus, Pseudomonas and Mycobacterium

Fungi → Aspergillus, Cephalosporium, Fusarium, Mucor, Penicillium, Rhizopus

Extracellular deoxyribonuclease is formed by the species of:

Bacteria → Arthrobacter, Bacillus, Clostridium, Pseudomonas

Fungi → Cladosporium, Fusarium

Schematic Pathway of decomposition of nucleic acid

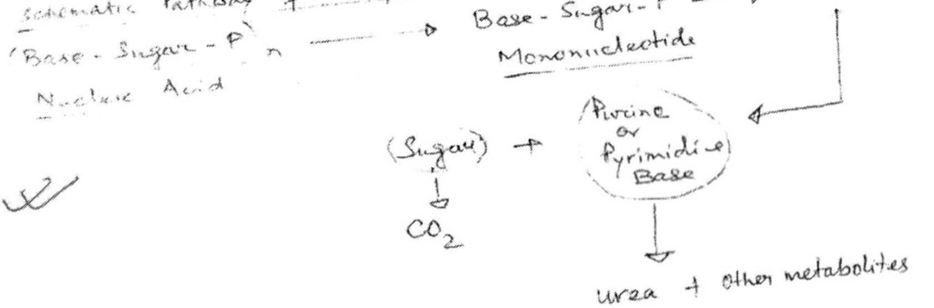

Decomposition of Urea

Many microorganisms possess the enzyme urease, the catalyst responsible for hydrolyzing urea.

$$CO(NH_2)_2 + H_2O \xrightarrow{\text{urease}} H_2NCOONH_4 \longrightarrow 2NH_3 + CO_2$$

urea Ammonium carbamate

Bacillus, Micrococcus, Pseudomonas, Klebsiella, Cyanobacterium, Clostridium and a diverse collection of fungi and actinomycetes use urea as a source of N for growth.

Urea bacteria are sensitive to acidic condition. They are absent or sparse in areas of pH 4.0 to 5.5. In acidic forest soil, the dominant urea-cleaving microflora are fungi.

FACTORS AFFECTING MINERALIZATION OF N — MART FIC

(i) Moisture: Organic N is mineralized at moderate or excessively high moisture levels. Ammonium is slowly formed at moisture levels slightly below the permanent wilting percentage, but improving the moisture status stimulates mineralization.

50-75% Ammonification occurs optimally between 50 and 75% of the water holding capacity.

Ammonification is not eliminated by soil submergence and the process is rapid in wet paddy fields where O_2 level is quite low. As a rule, soils active in aerobic mineralization also form NH_4^+ ion readily in the absence of O_2 and those slow in the process in aerated conditions likewise generate ammonium slowly under anaerobiosis. The final inorganic product, is, however, affected by the presence of O_2 as NH_4^+ ion is converted to nitrate only in well-aerated soils.

(ii) Alternate Wetting and Drying: Cycles of alternate wetting and drying, results in release of considerable quantities of the inorganic N from the organic N. But the rate of the process declines in the later cycles. Furthermore, the longer is the dry period, generally the greater is the amount of inorganic N released during the subsequent wet phase. Drying may cause disintegration or the cycle may make inaccessible substrates more easily available to the microflora. However, none of the explanations for this ammonium flush has enough supporting evidence.

(iii) Soil Reaction: Production of inorganic N ion (NH_4^+ + NO_3^-) is greater in neutral than in acid soils.

Neutral So, liming an acid soil is stimulatory to mineralization of organic N. Organic N accumulates in highly acid sites, presumably because of the slow mineralization, so that a rapid release is noted when such soils are limed.

(iv) Temperature: Temperature affects the mineralization sequence as each biochemical step is catalyzed by temperature-sensitive enzyme produced by the micro-organisms.

Thus, at 2°C, the microflora slowly mineralizes. From freezing to optimum temp, elevation of the temp enhances the mineralization in proportion to the greater warmth.

40-60°C

Optimum temperature for ammonification is not in the mesophilic range but rather it is above 40°C, usually between 40 and 60°C.

(v) Freezing ~~and Thaw~~ followed by thawing: It increases the mineralization of N

(vi) Addition of inorganic N: It sometimes enhances the mineralization of organic N.

(vii) Cultivation: Cultivation of virgin land promotes mineralization of organic N. So much inorganic N is released as ammonium ion, which is oxidized to nitrate.

$$\underset{\substack{\text{ammonia} \\ -3}}{NH_3} \xrightarrow{1/2\,O_2} \underset{\substack{\text{hydroxylamine} \\ -1}}{HO-NH_2} \xrightarrow{-2H} \frac{1}{2}\,\underset{\substack{\text{hyponitrite} \\ +1}}{HO-N=N-OH} \xrightarrow{1/2\,O_2} \underset{\substack{\text{nitrite} \\ +3}}{HO-N=O}$$

BIOCHEMISTRY OF NITRIFICATION

FIRST PHASE : Chemoautotrophs Nitrosomonas converts

$NH_4^+ \rightarrow NO_2^-$

Step 1 $NH_4^+ + \frac{1}{2}O_2 \xrightarrow{\text{oxidation}} NH_2OH + H^+$
Hydroxylamine

Nitrosomonas performs best at near pH 7.0 and NH_4^+ ion exists in soil at pH values near 7.0 and hydroxylamine is scarcely ionized at all.

Some part of the ammonia oxidation system may involve a copper enzyme. So, any Cu-enzyme poison, like, allyl thiourea, has a profound negative impact on ammonium oxidation.

Step 2 $NH_2OH + HNO_2 \longrightarrow NO_2 \cdot NH \cdot OH + 2[H]$
nitrohydroxylamine

Passed on either to the cytochrome system or to pyridine nucleotide carriers.

Step 3 $NO_2 \cdot NH \cdot OH + \frac{1}{2}O_2 \longrightarrow 2HNO_2$

This is a direct oxidation not involving any cytochrome system or auxiliary carriers.

The nitrite so formed passes into the medium in which the Nitrosomonas cells are growing.

Step 4, This step undoubtedly involves a cytochrome system

$2e^-$: $\overset{+3}{HNO_2} \rightarrow \overset{+5}{HNO_3}$

$NO_2^- \cdot H_2O + 2Cyt\,Fe^{3+} \xrightarrow{e^-\text{ removal (Oxdn)}} NO_3^- + 2Cyt\,Fe^{2+} + 2H^+$
Hydrated nitrite

$2Cyt\,Fe^{2+} + 2H^+ + \frac{1}{2}O_2 \xrightarrow{e^-\text{ gain (Redn)}} 2Cyt\,Fe^{3+} + H_2O$

This step must be accomplished by removal

of electrons ~~from nitrite~~ either from nitrite or from the water in which they are dissolved. This oxidation cannot take place by the addition of atmospheric Oxygen to nitrite because, if it did, cytochromes would not be involved.

BIOCHEMISTRY OF NITROGEN REDUCTION

Two different enzymatic pathways are involved in nitrate reduction.

1) Dissimilatory nitrate reduction: Through Dissimilatory nitrate reductase, organisms used the nitrate simply as an electron acceptor in place of O_2. Under more or less anaerobic conditions, microorganisms reduce nitrate to nitrite without assimilating it.

2) Assimilatory nitrate reductase: Through assimilatory nitrate reductase, microorganism reduce the nitrate to ammonia in order to tap it as a source of N for growth.

Nitrate reductase has several components.

$$PNH + H^+ + FAD \longrightarrow FADH_2 + PN^+$$

PNH: Reduced Pyridine nucleotide carrier; FAD: Oxidized Flavin Adenine dinucleotide; $FADH_2$: Reduced FAD; PN^+: Oxidized Pyridine nucleotide carrier

$$FADH_2 + 2\,Cyt\,Fe^{3+} \longrightarrow FAD + 2\,Cyt\,Fe^{2+} + 2H^+$$

$$2\,Cyt\,Fe^{2+} + 2H^+ + NO_3^- \xrightarrow{\text{(molybdenum enzyme)}} 2\,Cyt\,Fe^{3+} + NO_2^- + H_2O$$

Nitrite does not normally accumulate, because under anaerobic conditions it is itself further reduced either to ammonia or to nitrous oxide and nitrogen by the denitrifying bacteria.

Ammonia Production

$$2HNO_2 + 2[H] \longrightarrow NO_2 \cdot NH \cdot OH + H_2O$$

(Nitrite already formed) (Nitrohydroxyl amine)

$$NO_2 \cdot NH \cdot OH + 2[H] \longrightarrow HNO_2 + NH_2 \cdot OH$$

(HNO_2: Regeneration of HNO_2; $NH_2 \cdot OH$: Hydroxyl amine)

$$NH_2 \cdot OH + 2[H] \longrightarrow NH_3 + H_2O$$

Denitrification:

$$NO_2 \cdot NHOH + 2[H] \longrightarrow N_2O + 2H_2O$$

$$N_2O + 2[H] \longrightarrow N_2 + H_2O$$

Factors affecting denitrification

i) Oxygen and Redox Potential:

Generally, the rate of denitrification is inversely related to the O_2 concentration.

But losses of nitrogen under high aeration can usually be attributed to the existence of anaerobic microsites.

Denitrification occurs increasingly as the redox potential (E_h) drops below about +300 mV whereas during the reduction

NO_3^- + 200 — of NO_3^-, the E_h is poised at about +200 mV

NO_2^- 180 mV — whereas during nitrite reduction requires a E_h of about +180 mV. It would seem

100 mV Den. complete — that at about +100 mV, denitrification is complete.

(ii) Water Content: Denitrification occurs only at water contents greater than ~~a~~ about 60% of maximum water holding capacity. In flooded soils and sediments, the bulk of denitrification occurs at the soil-water interface with very little activity in water phase.

Soils ~~rich~~ which are water saturated but have a good aggregate ~~stability~~ structure may exhibit low denitrification because of the high inter-aggregate ~~structure~~ porosity and consequently high O_2 diffusion rate.

(iii) pH: The optimum pH for denitrification is between 7.0 and 8.0.
At low pH values, the mole fraction of N_2O increases and at about pH 4.0, N_2O may be the dominant product. However, the process is complicated at the lower pH values because of NO_2^- accumulation which is susceptible ~~are~~ to

a) enzymatic reduction (presumably through NO and N_2O to N_2)

b) Chemical decomposition ($3HNO_2 \rightarrow 2NO + HNO_3 + H_2O$)

Thus at low pH values, both NO and N_2O can be important products.

$Q_{10} = 2$

(iv) Temperature: Denitrification is temperature-dependent in the range 10 to 35°C, with a Q_{10} close to 2. At higher temperatures, the rate continues to increase, reaching a maximum in the region of 60 – 75°C and then declining rapidly to zero at higher temperatures. But it is not sure whether this phenomenon is due to activity of thermophilic organisms or an abiological reaction.

(v) Organic Carbon: The availability of electrons or reducing equivalents in organic ~~co~~ carbon compounds is one of the most important controlling factors governing the denitrifying activity of the heterotrophs which comprise the majority of denitrifiers.

It is consistent that soil denitrification rates are roughly proportional to the available C and that the process is usually stimulated by exogenous carbon.

Rates are most highly correlated with amounts of water-extractable organic C and of extractable reducing sugars.

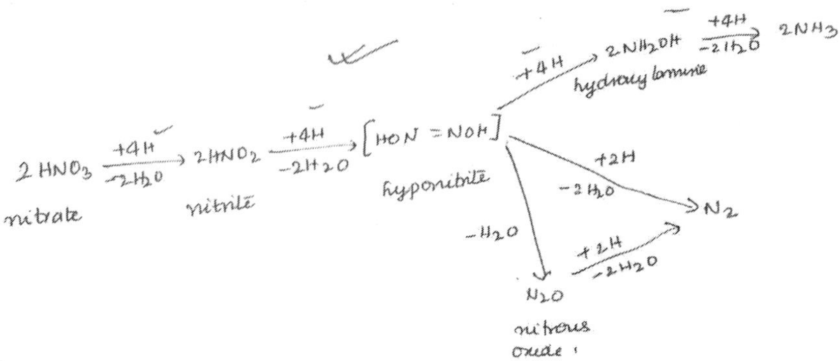

Biochemical pathway of nitrate reduction and denitrification

- For solution (dilute) like salt affected soil;

Debye-Hückel Limiting Law.

$$-\log \gamma_i = A z_i \sqrt{I}$$

so, $-\log \gamma_i \propto \sqrt{I}$.

- Bonding energy and ionic strength decrease with increase in distance.

(Coulomb's Inverse Square Law)

The magnitude of electrostatic attraction between 2 point charges $\propto$ multiplication of magnitude of charges

$\frac{1}{\propto}$ square of the distance between the charges.

$\therefore$ B.E $\propto$ I

$-\log \gamma_i \propto I$

$\Rightarrow$ BE $\propto -\log \gamma_i$.

- Adsorbability of cations :- Hofmeister series or Lyotrophic series

Monovalent : Ceruposolihy

$Cs^+ > Rb^+ > K^+ > Na^+ > Li^+ > H^+$

Divalent : Bastso calmag

$Ba^{2+} > Sr^{2+} > Ca^{2+} > Mg^{2+}$

Together : Alcal magpo amso

$Al^{3+} > Ca^{2+} > Mg^{2+} > K^+ = NH_4^+ > Na^+$.

THEORIES OF ION EXCHANGE

↳ ADSORPTION ISOTHERMS

equations showing adsorption of molecules or ions from the soil solution on the surfaces of soil solids.

- material adsorbed :- adsorbate
- material on which adsorption occurs :- adsorbent

eg. P adsorption of soil: cause of P-fixation
desorption :- slow and irreversible
- cause large hysteresis effect

Adsorbed NH_4^+ ions ⇒ less susceptible to nitrification.

- The amount of adsorbate per unit mass of adsorbent depends on :-
  a) nature of the adsorbate
  b) ,, ,, ,, adsorbent
  c) concentration of adsorbate at equil^m ~~and temp~~.
  d) temperature.

- Mathematically,

bate ↗

$$\frac{x}{m} = f\,(\text{nature of adsorbent, adsorbate, C, T})$$

bent ↙

- when adsorbent is in contact with adsorbate, adsorption ~~occurs gradu~~ increases.
- Then, when amount of adsorbate is less in the soln, desorption ↓ maintain equilibrium.
- Adsorption data at equil^m is reported in form of ad. isotherm ↙ - plot between amt of adsorbate ~~and~~ per unit mass of adsorbent and the equil^m conc^n of adsorbate at constant temp.

- Different equations to predict shapes of the isotherms.

laq nib ↳ Freundlich (1926)
laq lag ↳ Langmuir (1918)
laq mog ↳ Brunaer et al (1938)

→ Langmuir (1918)
Freundlich (1926)
BET (1938).

LANGMUIR ADSORPTION THEORY

- Basic theory of adsorption of gases on solids.
- assumptions

i) surface of solid → adsorption site → can adsorb one gas molecule → if another hits, deflected back.

ii) all sites have same affinity for that gas molecule

iii) presence of a gas molecule on one site → doesn't affect the properties of the neighbouring sites.

iv) rate of adsorption ∝ no. of adsorption sites, pressure of gas

rate of desorption ∝ no. of occupied sites.

Linear form of equation

$$\frac{c}{x} = \frac{C}{x_m} + \frac{1}{x_m k}.$$

rate of condensation = rate of evaporation = said to be in equil^m.

C = equilibrium conc^n of the adsorbate
x = amt adsorbed per unit mass of adsorbent
x_m = max^m amt adsorbed . . . . . . as a monolayer
k = equil^m constant related to bonding energy.

- Experimental adsorption data

c/x versus c.

slope = $\frac{1}{x_m}$

intercept = $\frac{1}{x_m k}$

slope = steepness

intercept = value of y at the point where the lines cross Y-axis.

isotherm = between amt adso per unit mass and concentration.

- However a liner plot of data – not sufficient for obeying Langmuir Eq.

↓

Khasawnch and Copeland (1973) lagtime

↓

supply parameter (SP)

(including constants and coeff. from Lang)

$$SP = \sqrt{\frac{qc}{x_m k}}$$

$q = x$.

→ X_m can be found out from the slope of c/x vs c.

↓

→ ~~Specific~~ surface area (A) of soil

$$A = \frac{X_m N \pi r^2}{M}$$

$X_m = g$

N = number of molecules mol^{-1}

r = radius of adsorbate molecule

M = molecular wt ($g\ mol^{-1}$)

If adsorbate = gas.

X_m → replaced → volume of the gas reqd to form a mono layer (V_m)

M → volume occupied by a mole.

(22.4 litre at 273 K)

$$\text{ie } A = \frac{V_m\,(cm^3)\, N \pi r^2}{22400\ (cm^3\ mol^{-1})}$$

→ Normally, Languir not used to calculate A.

as it ~~do~~

Limitations

- not used to calculate A normally as not define total adsorption process but a certain fraction.
- soils (mixtures of inorganic and organic)
  - ↳ so the idea of identical sites is limited.
  - ↳ no change of sites theory.
- too restrictive for cation exchange equilibria → as doesn't take into account of the competiting ions.
- refers adsorption of gases on non-ionic solid. But soil → ionic process.

FREUNDLICH ISOTHERM (1926)

- originally an empirical equation
- ~~but~~ implies that B.E of the adsorbate decreases with fractional coverage of the surface area of the adsorbent.
- most widely used equation to describe experimental data on adsorption.
- But not used for predicting maxm adsorption

So, mathematically,

$$x = Kc^n \quad (n < 1)$$

Linear form →

$$\log x = \log K + n \log c.$$

plot between ~~x and c~~ → log x and log c.

$$y = mx + c$$

$$\Rightarrow \log x = n \log c + \log K.$$

slope = n

intercept = $\log K$.

BRUNAER, EMMETT AND TELLER (BET)

– For langmuir equation
↳ independent on pressure after formation of monolayer.

→ So, it fails for those gases at higher pressures because more than a monolayer of adsorbed molecules ~~are~~ is formed.

→ BET → extension of Langmuir for multilayer adsorption

→ assumptions

i) Heat of adsorption in 2nd, 3rd, nth layer = ... monolayer.

ii) If adsorption ⇒ on free surface, then at p^0 (saturation pressure of the gas), an infinite no. of layers can be built up on the adsorbent.

Linear form:

$$\frac{p}{v(p^0 - p)} = \frac{(c'-1)p}{V_m c' p^0} + \frac{1}{V_m c'}$$

p = any equil^m pressure

v = x.

V_m = Xm.

c' = constant at a given temp.

→ $\frac{p}{v(p^0-p)}$ vs $\frac{p}{p^0}$.

→ slope = $\frac{(c'-1)}{V_m c'}$

intercept = $\frac{1}{V_m c'}$

Advantages

- describes the multilayer adsorption
- can calculate surface area → Disadvantage
- can yield vol. of gas reqd to form a monolayer.

BET – most useful between relative pressure (P/p_0)
0.05 – 0.45.

→ V_m × cross sectional area of adsorbate = surface area.

Disadvantage

- Weakly adsorbed molecules like N → may not penetrate in all the layers.
- Strongly adsorbed like NH_3 → int- penetrate internal surface area

→ underestimation and overestimation of surface area.

HYSTERESIS

- adsorptions of ions by colloidal surface by ionic – interactions are desorbed by expenditure of same energy that was released during adsorption.
- However, for ligand exchange processes – such as those in P – fixation, SO_4^{2-} – fixation and also for cation K^+ (sorbed in interlayer space) → desorption requires much more energy → as retentive forces are covalent.

↓

irreversibility of adsorption – desorption process.

↓

Hysteris effect.

- H.E in K^+ depends on → amount of illitic materials
→ state of weathering ↑ → H.E ↓.

ELECTRICAL DIFFUSE DOUBLE LAYER THEORY

Assumptions

- charged particle has flat surface without edge effect
- exchange sites are uniformly dist. over the entire planar surface
- Dielectric cons. of water in aqueous soln phase is constant.
- ions act as point charges
- interaction between ions is negligible but interaction between ion and charged surface is electrostatically
- charge on the surface neutralized by the excess of oppositely charged ions.

→ For a mixture of monovalent and divalent ions

↓

Gouy-Chapman theory of the diffuse double layer.

→ Fractional saturation of the exchange complex by monovalent ion depends on—

- surface charge density of exchanger
- cationic composition of the equiln soln.
- interaction between diffuse dou. layer on the adjacent clay platelets.

↓

Simplified form (Bolt, 1955)

$$\frac{\Gamma^+}{\Gamma} = \frac{r}{\Gamma\sqrt{\beta}} \sinh^{-1} \frac{\Gamma\sqrt{\beta}}{r + 4V_d\sqrt{C_2}}$$

Γ = total surface charge density (mol/m²)

Γ^+/Γ = fraction of total surface neutralized by monovalent cation,

C_1 = Equilm concn of monov. cation (mol L⁻¹)

C_2 - - - - - divalent

$r = \frac{C_1}{\sqrt{C_2}}$ $\left(\frac{\sqrt{mol}}{\sqrt{L}}\right)$ reduced ratio of monovalent cation

Ψ_d = cos Ψ_d – electrical pot at midway plane between two adjacent clay platelets

β = 1.08 × 10¹⁵ m mol⁻¹ at 29

$$\frac{\Gamma^+}{\Gamma} = \frac{r}{\Gamma\sqrt{\beta}} \sinh^{-1} \frac{\Gamma\sqrt{\beta}}{r + 4V_d\sqrt{C_2}}$$

Thickness of diffuse double layer, defined by δ (delta)

$$\delta = \left[\frac{\varepsilon k T}{2 n_0 Z^2 e^2}\right]^{1/2}$$

ε = Epsilon
= static permittivity of the medium
(dielectric constant)

K = Boltzmann constant
= $1.38 \times 10^{-23}\ m^2\ kg\ s^{-2} K^{-1} / JK^{-1}$.
(named after Ludwig Boltzmann)
= physical constant relating energy at the individual particle level with temperature
= $\frac{R}{N_A}$ R – gas constant, N_A – Avogadro's constant

T = Absolute temperature
= ~~(0K)~~ = 298 K.
= ~~at~~ system in ~~lowest~~ /min^m^ energy.

e = electron charge = 1.602×10^{-19} C.

n_0 = no. of ions per m^3 in the equil^m^ solution = $C_0 \times 10^3 \times 6.022 \times 10^{23}$

Z = numerical value of the valency of the counter ion (cation in case of -vely charged surface)

→ $\varepsilon = \varepsilon_0 D$ ↳ Dielectric constant (78.5 at 298 K for H_2O)
↓
permittivity in vacuum ($8.85 \times 10^{-12}\ C^2 J^{-1} mol^{-1}$)

$$\delta = \left[\frac{\varepsilon K T}{2 n_0 Z^2 e^2}\right]^{1/2} = \frac{3 \times 10^{-10}}{Z}\left(\frac{1}{C_0}\right)^{1/2} m.$$

$$= \frac{3}{Z (C_0)^{1/2}}\ A^0 \text{ or}$$

C_0 = conc^n^ of the equilibrium soln (mol L^{-1})

For 1:1 electrolyte i.e ($Z = 1, C_0 = 0.1$ mol L^{-1}) $\delta = 1$ nm.

while at $C_0 = 0.001$ mol L^{-1}, $\delta = 10$ nm.

FACTORS AFFECTING THE THICKNESS OF DIFFUSE DOUBLE LAYER (δ)

- TOTAL ELECTROLYTE CONCENTRATION (TEC)

Electrolyte ↑ → layer ↓.

→ ↑ 4 times → ↓ 2 times.

TUDT

VALENCE OF THE COUNTER ION.

Valency ↑ → layer ↓.

→ at a fixed electrolyte concentration ∴ the thickness of D.D.L for divalent ions would be 1/2 than that of monovalent

- DIELECTRIC CONSTANT

Diele. constant ↑ → Thickness ↑.

TEMPERATURE

Temp ↑ → Dielectric constant ↓ → Thickness ↓.

due to a higher kinetic energy of the counter ions.

DONNAN MEMBRANE EQUILIBRIUM

If an aqueous soln of an electrolyte with two diffusible ions (one cation one anion) is separated - by a membrane from another solution con with non-diffusible ions → then the ionic distribution of the diff ions at equilibrium → the ionic distribution of the diff ions on both sides unequal → even ionic proactivity product of equivalent amounts of oppositely charged or ratio of equivalent amounts of like-charged ions on two sides will be equal.

→ membrane of selective permeability is Donnan membrane.

→ However, NaCl of concn C_1 separated with NaCl of concn C_2 where $C_2 > C_1$.

At equilibrium

(L)	M	(R)
$Na^+ Cl^-$ (C_1)		$Na^+ Cl^-$ (C_2)
$Na^+ R^-$		

$$(C_{Na^+})_L = (C_{Na^+})_R$$

$$(C_{Cl^-})_L = (C_{Cl^-})_R.$$

$$\Rightarrow (C_{Na^+})_L (C_{Cl^-})_L = (C_{Na^+})_R (C_{Cl^-})_R. \quad \text{——(1)}$$

However, if in another soln a salt with non-diffusible ion is introduced—

$$(C_{Na^+})_R = (C_{Cl^-})_R$$

$$(C_{Na^+})_L = (C_{Cl^-})_L + (C_{R^-})_L$$

$\Rightarrow$ From equation (1)

$$(C_{Na^+})_L (C_{Cl^-})_L = (C_{Na^+})_R (C_{Cl^-})_R.$$

$$\Rightarrow [(C_{Cl^-})_L + (C_{R^-})_L](C_{Cl^-})_L = (C_{Cl^-})_R^2$$

$$\Rightarrow (C_{Cl^-})_L^2 + (C_{R^-})_L (C_{Cl^-})_L = (C_{Cl^-})_R^2$$

$$\Rightarrow (C_{Cl^-})_R \neq (C_{Cl^-})_R$$

$$\Rightarrow (C_{Na^+})_L \neq (C_{Na^+})_R.$$

In a diffuse double layer, → exists a terminal end of solution side dominated by anions.
↳ considered as a donnan membrane.

→ considering K^+, Ca^{2+} and Cl^- →
at equilibrium

$$(C_{K^+})_{exch}\,(C_{Cl^-})_{exch} = (C_{K^+})_{soln}\,(C_{Cl^-})_{soln}$$

$$(C_{Ca^{2+}})_{exch}\,(C_{Cl^-})^2_{exch} = (C_{Ca^{2+}})_{soln}\,(C_{Cl^-})^2_{soln}$$

KCl.
$Ca^{2+}Cl$.

Combining →

$$\frac{(C_{K^+})_{exch}}{(C_{K^+})_{soln}} = \frac{(C_{Cl^-})_{soln}}{(C_{Cl^-})_{exch}} = \sqrt{\frac{(C_{Ca^{2+}})_{exch}}{(C_{Ca^{2+}})_{soln}}}$$

ie

$$\frac{C_{K^+}}{\sqrt{C_{Ca^{2+}}}}_{exch} = \frac{C_{K^+}}{\sqrt{C_{Ca^{2+}}}}_{soln}$$

↳ any dilution → release of K^+. (vice versa for divalent ion).

CATION EXCHANGE EQUATIONS BASED ON LAW OF MASS ACTION

- formulations – relationships between cations in the solution and adsorbed phases at equilibrium : cation ex. equations

Assumptions

- freely accessible exchange sites to soln cations
- constant surface charge.
- homogeneous adsorbed phase
- anions excluded from monolayer of cations
- no chelation in surface.

Homovalent cation exchange equilibria

$$A^{z+}_{soil} + B^{z+}_{soln} \rightleftharpoons B^{z+}_{soil} + A^{z+}_{soln}.$$

eg. $Na^{+}_{soil} + K^{+}_{soln} \rightleftharpoons Na^{+}_{soln} + K^{+}_{soil}.$

However, K^{+}_{soil} doesn't imply that entire amount of exc. Na^{+} is replaced.

Law of Mass action

$$K_m = \frac{[B^{z+}_{soil}]\,(A^{z+}_{soln})}{[A^{z+}_{soil}]\,(B^{z+}_{soln})}$$

[ ] → activity of ex. ion in adsorbed.
( ) → soln.

→ derived by Kerr (1928) laqnag and Vanselow (1932) laqman
↳ under assumption solid phase is an ideal solid solution.

→ Km = selectivity constant or Quotient.
→ But mostly applicable to homovalent ion exchange system
→ Gapon (1933) laqmam → considered also → ideal solid soln. but with heterovalent systems → more practical.

→ Gapon use ionic concn.

$$Z_B A^{z+}_{A\,soil} + Z_A B^{z+}_{B\,soln} \rightleftharpoons Z_A B^{z+}_{B\,soil} + Z_B A^{z+}_{A\,soln}.$$

$$(Z_A^{+} \neq Z_B^{+})$$

According to Kerr-Vanselow equation:

$$K_m = \frac{[B^{z+}_{B}\,soil]^{Z_A}\,(A^{z+}_{A}\,soln)^{Z_B}}{[A^{z+}_{A}\,soil]^{Z_B}\,(B^{z+}_{B}\,soln)^{Z_A}}$$

According to Gapon,

If $2Na^{+}_{soil} + Ca^{2+}_{soln} \rightleftharpoons Ca^{2+}_{soil} + 2Na^{+}_{soln}$;

Ca^{2+} ion saturation =

$Ca^{2+}_{soil} = CEC - Na^{+}_{soil}$

So, According to Gapon,

$$K_G(K_m) = \frac{[CEC - A_A^{Z+}soil]\,(A_A^{Z+}soln)^{1/Z_A}}{[A_A^{Z+}soil]_B\,(B_B^{Z+}soln)^{1/Z_B}}$$

eg. $2Na^{+}_{soil} + Ca^{2+}_{soln} \rightleftharpoons Ca^{2+}_{soil} + 2Na^{+}_{soln}$.

Dividing both sides by 2,

$Na^{+}_{soil} + \frac{1}{2}Ca^{2+}_{soln} \rightleftharpoons \frac{1}{2}Ca^{2+}_{soil} + Na^{+}_{soln}$.

$$K_G = \frac{[Ca^{2+}_{soil}]^{1/2}\,(Na^{+}_{soln})}{[Na^{+}]_{soil}\,(Ca^{2+}_{soln})^{1/2}}$$

$$K_G = \frac{[CEC - Na^{+}_{soil}]\,(Na^{+}_{soln})}{[Na^{+}_{soil}]\,(Ca^{2+}_{soln})^{1/2}}$$

→ If Km were a thermodynamic equilm constant
↳ its values must be constant with the position of the equilibriu.

→ in heterovalent → more variations of Km.
↳ due to the assumption of ideal solid solution behaviour.

lag some

THERMODYNAMIC THEORY (GAINES AND THOMAS, 1953)

- fugacity → escaping tendency of a gas in a mixture.

→ $f/c = 1$ (for all values in ideal solⁿ)
↳ concentration

$\lim_{c \to 0} f/c = 1$ (for non-ideal solution)

$a = f/f_0$ → fugacity in the standard state (of unit activity)

↓ activity of a solⁿ in a binary solⁿ.

- Standard state of a solute
  - is when activity is one for the solute
  - behaves ideally at 1 molar, 1 molal or 1 mole fraction concn.

such concn is too concentrated to behave ideally

so it is just hypothetical

→ Ideal behaviour may be expected in dilute soln 10^{-4} - 10^{-5} M.

GAINES AND THOMAS THEORY OF CATION EXCHANGE IN SOIL

$$Z_B A^{Z+}_{A\,soil} + Z_A B^{Z+}_{B\,soln} \rightleftharpoons Z_B A^{Z+}_{A\,soln} + Z_A B^{Z+}_{B\,soil}$$

c = +ve soln
q = −ve exchange

Selectivity coefficient.

$$K_m/K_c = \frac{(q_B/q_0)^{Z_A}\,(C_A/C_0)^{Z_B}}{(q_A/q_0)^{Z_B}\,(C_B/C_0)^{Z_A}} \cdot \frac{\gamma A^{Z_B}}{\gamma B^{Z_A}} \quad C_0\,B\,B\cdot A^{(Z-Z)}$$

q_B = Equivalent −ve sites occupied by B^+ ions on exchange phase
q_A = " " " " A^+ ions on " "
q_0 = Total no. of equivalent −ve sites " " " "
C_0 = Total equivalent +ve sites " " " " site
C_A = Equivalent +ve sites in soln occupied by A^+
C_B = " " " "

γ_A = activity coeff of A^+ ion in soln phase at equiln
γ_B = " " " " B^+ ion.

C_A/C_0 = Mole fraction of A^+
C_B/C_0 = " " " "

- So K_M / K_c → not a thermodynamic equil^m constant
- <u>assumptions of Gaines & Thomas</u>
  - adsorbed ionic layer treated as solid soln (not ideal)
    ↳ so that ~~ionic~~ cationic conc^n can be obtained from the fraction of the total ion sites on exchange phase → occupied by cations.
    (<u>fractional saturation of</u> CEC
- standard <u>state of</u> unit <u>activity</u> of an <u>adsorbed</u> cation
  ↳ is when all ionic sites are fully saturated by the cation concerned and behaves ideally so that $a_+ = c_+ = 1$.

  ∴ Bonding energy
  $$(B.E)_+ \propto -\log f_+ = 0.$$

CLAY-MEMBRANE ELECTRODE AND IONIC ACTIVITY

- direct method for ionic activity measurement
  - ↳ developed by Marshall by way of using a clay membrane electrodes for → activities of Na^+, K^+, Mg^{2+}, Ca^{2+}, Ba^+ with a saturated calomel electrode
    - ↳ reference el.

- clay membrane — reversible to → cations
  - → monovalent cations only.
  - ↓ lack of specificity → limited to homoionic system
    - → systems cont. monovalent and divalent cations.

→ Marshall and his coworkers (1940) lagrod
  - ↳ determine ionic activity as a function of
    - → degree of saturation
    - → degree of ionization of exc ions
    - → mean free bonding energy (ΔG_m)

→ For a monovalent cation, M^+.

$$\Delta G_M = RT \ln \frac{C_M}{a_M}$$

- C_M — Concⁿ of total monoval. cation (Σ of ionized + non-ionize.)
- a_M → activity of the monovalent cation.
- R ↓ Universal Gas Constant
- T → absolute temperature.

we also have,

$$a_m = f_m \cdot C_m$$

↳ activity coeff.

$$\Delta G_m = RT \ln \frac{C_m}{f_m \cdot C_m} = -RT \ln f_m = RT \ln f_m^{-1}$$

- Marshall termed f_m → fraction active
  - ↙ fraction accessible to ionic activity measurement by clay membrane electrode.

KRISHNAMOORTHY - DAVIS - OVERSTREET EQUATION (1948)

SCHOFIELD'S RATIO LAW

- if a -ve -vely charged surface → equi^lm → sol^n phase containing monovalent, divalent and trivalent cations

↓

the equi^lm will not be disturbed if the activities of the monovalent cations in the solution phase are altered by a factor

↳ of the divalent cations by square of the factor

↳ of the trivalent cations by cube of the factor

→ In other words,

in binary system (two cations) —

the ratio of the cations held by a soil depends upon—

a) ratio of acti. of two cations in equil^n sol^n.

(in case of homovalent cations)

b) ratio of activity of monovalent / square root of act of divalent

(in case of mono-divalent cations)

c) ratio of ac. of monovalent / cube root of act of trivalent.

and so on.,

→ no exchange of cations so long as a_{Na}/a_K, $a_{Na}/(a_{Ca})^{1/2}$, $a_{Na}/(a_{Al})^{1/3}$ donot alter for Na^+-K^+, Na^+-Ca^{2+} and Na^+-Al^{3+} binary sy.

APPLICATION OF SCHOFIELD RATIO LAW

Say, in a binary solution system, at equil^m.

$$K^+_{soil} + \frac{1}{2}Ca^{2+}_{soln} \rightleftharpoons K^+_{soln} + \frac{1}{2}Ca^{2+}_{soil}$$

$$K = \frac{[Ca^{2+}_{soil}]^{1/2}(K^+_{soln})}{[K^+_{soil}](Ca^{2+}_{soln})^{1/2}}$$

$$\Rightarrow \frac{[K^+_{soil}]}{[Ca^{2+}_{soil}]^{1/2}} = \frac{(K^+_{soln})}{(Ca^{2+}_{soln})^{1/2}} = 1/2 = (say) = K.$$

On irrigation, the concentration is diluted and is decreased to 4 fold.

$$\Rightarrow \quad 1/2 \times 1/2 = 1/4.$$

But equil^m demands the value of $K = 1/2$ to remain constant as long as temperature is constant.

to keep $K = 1/2$, there will be redistribution of ions.

↓

release of K^+ ions from adsorbed to solution and adsorption of Ca^{2+} ions to adsorbed.

- Appropriate steps to increase the K^+ conc^n in soln phase (by MOP application) such a way that

↓

while Ca^{2+} ion conc in soln is diluted 4 times

K^+ - - - - - - - - only 2 times. $\sqrt{4} = 2$

$$\frac{[K^+_{soil}]}{[Ca^{2+}_{soil}]^{1/2}} = \frac{(K^+_{soln}/2)}{(Ca^{2+}_{soln}/4)^{1/2}} = 1/2 \text{ (constant)}.$$

↳ equil^m is not disturbed.

↳ similar conclusions may be derived from D.M. Equilibrium.

$$\left[\frac{a_{K^+}}{\sqrt{a_{Ca^{2+}}}}\right]_{\substack{exch \\ or\ adso}} = \left[\frac{a_{K^+}}{\sqrt{a_{Ca^{2+}}}}\right]_{soln}$$

- ~~wt~~ Irrigation a soil with brackish H_2O → high concn of Na^+.

so, Na^+ ⟶ solution ⟶ increase ESP.
Ca^{2+}, Mg ⟶ adsorped ↓ poor soil tilth.

To counter the effect, pre treatment of the irrigation source with gypsum → increase Ca^{2+} ion → check rise of ESP.
↓
no shift in position of equilibrium
↓
risk of sodification avoided.

INVERSE RATIO LAW

- considers disturbance in equilibrium position.
↓
due to extraneous factors
due to change in concn of ions.

- Monovalent ions → found more in no in low charge density exchange phase of a colloid (ie dilute phase)
- Reverse is for divalent ions.

Reason

ionic fields of the monovalent cations — more compatible with ionic fields of the low ~~cho~~ CEC clays.

for divalent → high CEC clays.

eg. If aqueous dispersions of kaolinite and mont clay are mixed → allowed to stand in equilibrium
↓
Monovalent ions → found more on exchange phase of kaolinite.

PLANT ROOT EXCHANGE IN SOIL

- plant roots → feeble (weak) ion exchangers in soil
  - ↳ due to feeble net -ve charge on it.
- uptake cations in exchange of secretion of equivalent quantity of H^+.
  - ↳ so rhizospheric pH lower than bulk soil pH
- anion uptake in exchange for equivalent amt of OH^-/HCO_3^-
- imbalance in cation/anion uptake by the plant
  - ↳ results net -ve charge.
  - electrical double layer at the root-soil soln interface.
- Monocots (cereals) lower root CEC than dicot (legumes)
  - ↳ behave like kaolinetic — montmo.
  - ↳ preferrance of monovalent ions — divalent.

eg. K^+ deficiency more in plot of rice + maize than rice + berseem } no potash application.

	Kaolinite	fine mica	Smectite
SSA (Specific surface area) – $m^2 g^{-1}$	5 – 20	100-120	700-800
SCD (Surface charge density) – $mol\ m^{-2}$	6.7×10^{-6}	1.65×10^{-6}	1.25×10^{-6}

FACTOR AFFECTING CATION EXCHANGE CAPACITY:-

- SOIL FACTORS.
- Effect of clay Minerals

  Smectite > fine mica > kaolinite

- Effect of OM

  → two opposite effects

i) closed spaced carboxyl and phenolic groups cause ↑ in SCD of soil → selectivity towards multivalent cations

ii) increase of internal/external surface area / exchange sites
  ↳ increases preferance of exchanger for monovalent cations.

Surface charge density

- diffuse double layer equation
  - ↳ higher SCD of soil – smaller the fractional saturation of soil-exchange complex by monovalent cation in mono-divalent system.

However fails to predict exchange behaviour of soils when monovalent cation
  - ↳ strongly affected by geometry of exchange sites

SOLUTION FACTORS

- Total electrolyte concentration (TEC)

Preferance for divalent ↑ → ↑ in ~~electroly~~ TEC.

- Type of cations

Of same valency but diff hydrated size.
  - ↳ specificity for exchange sites.

In Ca-Mg system → Ca over Mg.

- Type of anions
- eqn. don't take the nature of anions.
- formation of more stronger ion-pairs by divalent anions with divalent cations as compared to monovalent cation influence mono-divalent cation exchange equilⁿ.

NEGATIVE ADSORPTION

↓

Interaction of anions with the clay particles

↓ bonding of the anions by the +ve charges (broken edges)

→ repulsion between anions and -ve charges on the planar surface.

↓

cause a deficit of anions near a clay particle

↓

called as negative adsorption

↳ shown by all soils at to a certain extent.

VOLUME OF EXCLUSION AND ESTIMATION OF SPECIFIC SURFACE AREA OF SOIL.

- Volume of exclusion :- volume completely free of anions.

↳ Equivalent distance of exclusion × specific surface area
(δdl, cm)

→ ~~Volume ↓ → ↑~~.

→ volume of exclusion ↑ → ↓ in TEC

→ " " " ↑ → ↑ in SSA

→ Volume of exclusion × equil^{m} concn of the anion (meq ml^{-1})
= amt of anion excluded per unit mass of soil.

→ fraction of liquid layer free of anion ↑ → ↓ in moisture content

→ If equivalent exclusion distance is a non-negligible part of liquid layer (dl, cm) → following aspects involved

(1) anions move faster than mean flow velocity.
↳ = Darcy velo. / water-filled porosity.

Reason :- Salt soln flows through pores.
↳ anion exclusion near the walls of pores occurs
↳ increase in velocity of liquid with increase in distance from the colloid surface.

b) Because of anion exclusion.
concn of anions in easily extractable soil solution becomes higher than that in soil soln obtained by means of high pressure filtration.

ANION EXCHANGE

Law of Mass action
Cato M. Guldberg
Peter Wage

Rate of reaction ∝ Product of concentration of participating molecules.

SOIL COLLOIDS

D.K. DAS

NATURE AND PROPERTIES OF SOIL COLLOIDS

i) Adsorption

- adsorption of ions governed by nature of the ion and type of colloidal particle.
- ↑ valency, more strongly adsorbed.
- H^+ → act as polyvalent ion → so more strongly adsorbed than divalent.
- kaolinitic clay – greater anion fixation (eg. $H_2PO_4^-$ fixation).

ii) Brownian movement

- colloidal particles – continual motion
  - ↳ due to collision of colloidal particles in the dispersion medium
  - ↳ responsible for coagulation or flocculation.

iii) Electrical charge. –

- some -ve and some +ve.

iv) Flocculation

colloidal particles flocculate by addition of oppositely charged ion.

clay floc → Al^{3+}, H^+, Ca^{2+} (humid & sub humid), Na^+ → arid regions.

↳ important for good soil structure.

$Al^{3+} > Ca^{2+}$ and $H^+ > Mg^{2+} > K^+ \geq NH_3^+ > Na^+$

v) Plasticity

- > 15 % of colloidal clay exhibits
- moist or wet.
- molded to any shape.

vi) Cohesion and adhesion.

cohesion → clay form aggregates
adhesion → clay envelope sand.
} → helps in retention of H_2O ~~as well as nutrients~~.

vii) Swelling and shrinkage

↳ imbibition of H_2O ↳ dry condition

- ~~more~~ pronounced in montmorillonite

viii) Non-permeability

- unable to pass semipermeable membrane.

TYPES OF SOIL COLLOIDS

- Individual crystalline particle - micelle or micro cell.
- Colloidal clay → neither lyophilic nor lyophobic.

surface tension & viscosity similar to disp. medium. → intermediate.

Hydrophilic → because of its hydration

hydrophobic → sensitivity to electrolytes

↓ s.t & viscosity.

LYOPHOBIC	LYOPHILIC
i) surface tension and viscosity ~~a~~ similar to dispersion medium	i) lower.
ii) Small quantities of electrolyte cause precipitation	ii) Large.
iii) easily detect in ultra microscope	iii) not easily
iv) move in one direction in an electric field	iv) diff. directions.

SILICATE CLAYS

~~Sf~~ I) Size and chemical composition

↳ < 2µm Silica, Al, Fe, Combined H_2O.

ii) Shape.
Laminated – layers of plates

iii) Surface area
area accessible to ions → in aqueous solution.
external surface area
internal surface area

iv) Electronegative charges
-ve charges
– inner ionic layer (-ve charges.
– outer ionic layer (cations swarming layer)

v) Adsorbed cations
- determine the physical and chemical properties of the soil – influence plant growth.
eg. alkali soil dominated by Na^+.

AMORPHOUS CLAYS

- aluminosilicate
- not well-oriented crystals.
- not minerals technically (due to no crystallinity)
- volcanic ash.
- inconsistent properties.
- almost all of their charges is from –OH ions → gain H^+ ion or lose H^+ attached.
- variable charge.

SESQUIOXIDE CLAYS (METAL OXIDES AND HYDROUS OXIDES)

– extensive rainfall → leaching and weathering in humid warm climates → silica and aluminium leach away →
↳ remnant → low solubilities

– mixtures of aluminium hydroxide, $Al(OH)_3$ and iron oxide Fe_2O_3 or fe hydroxide $Fe(OH)_3$.

– $Al_2O_3 \cdot xH_2O$
$Fe_2O_3 \cdot xH_2O$

- don't swell.
- doesn't behave like silicate clays.

FERTILIZERS, MANURES AND BIOFERTILIZERS

- materials containing one or more nutrient elements in form of chemical compounds of organic or inorganic nature
- natural deposit / industrially synthesized.
- on application to soil, dissolve fully or sparingly
- some undergo chemical transformation.

HISTORY OF MANURING IN ANCIENT INDIA

- documented in Vedas and Upanishads
- moreover, green manure & wood ash — Medieval period.
- traditional knowledge
- benefits of fallowing, mixed cropping or crop rotation
- 1805 AD — to set up experimental farms in Lower Bengal (Bihar & Orissa) (proposal) lagdose
- came up at Barrackpore f. 6 Pusa in Bihar.
- Famine Enquiry Commission 1866 → suggested lagbobb → Agricult. Dept.
- lagguna 1882 - Imperial & Provincial Ag. depts established.
- first expert appointed
- Agricultural Research Institute at Pusa — renamed — Imperial Ag. Research Institute at 1905. lagdose
- ↳ Dr J.W Leather - first Imperial Ag. chemist in India.
  - ↳ Father of Soil Sc and Ag. chem in India.
- Nitrogen received special attention first.
- Use of fert in Indian Ag → 1950s. lagsod

FERTILIZERS IN INDIAN AGRI.

- 1965-66 → Green Revo. started.
- Fert. usage ↑.
- 2009 → 2nd consumer of fert. N, P (after china).
  - 3rd " " K (after china, USA)

FERTILISER (CONTROL) ORDER

- 2006 — legally enforceable by executive orders
  - issued by Govt. of India under Essential Commodities Act, 1955. passed by Parliament.
- came into force. - 1957. lagshoobing

- includes two schedules (I and II) besides Forms of Registration and Appendices.

Schedule I :→ specifications Part A
max nutrient content
" moisture "
physical parameter

tolerance limits Part B

Schedule II : – procedures for drawal of samples of fertilizers. Part A
detailed methods of analysis of fert. Part B

HISTORY OF FERTILIZER PRODUCTION

GLOBAL SCENE

- Ground bone as fertilizer → United States of Am. → 1825 lagnose
- Peruvian guano ($NaNO_3$) → German botanist – Humboldt – ~~1840~~ 1802 lagdon
- Patent to manufacture Superphosphate – John B. Lawes – 1842 lag
  lagnum ↳ Produced in 1843
  ↳ treating coprolites (fossilized dung) + H_2SO_4.
  first commercially venture of fert. production
- Mining of phosphate rock in USA – 1868. lagbog
  in North Am – 1899. lag99
- Mixed fert – USA – 1849 lagreq

DEVELOPMENTS IN INDIA

- first fertilizer single superphosphate → 1906 lagdobe
  → also mixtures.

→ $NH_4(SO_4)_2$ – byproduct of steel industry → 1933. lagmum

– Reference

Year	Fertilizer	Manufacturer
1906	— Single superphosphate	EID - Parry (India) Ltd, Ranipet
1906	— Fert mixtures	
	Ammonium sulphate	
1933	a) as by-product of steel industry	
1941	b) using H_2SO_4.	
1947	c) using gypsum as raw material	
1974	d) as a by-product of polymer/ caprolactum	
1959	Ammonium sulphate nitrate (ASN)	FCI Ltd, Sindri
1959	Urea	
	Ammonium chloride (NH_4Cl)	
1960	Ammonium phosphate	
1961	CAN	
1965	Nitrophosphate	
1967	DAP	
1968	TSP	
	Urea ammonium phosphate (UAP)	
	NPK complex.	
1973	Pelofos	

FAI – FERTILISER ASSOCIATION OF INDIA

– 1955
– national representative body of all fert. manufacturers in India.
– functions
- bridge between fert industry & Govn.
- close liaison with international bodies.
- provides fora for exchange of views.
- studies on specific topics
- clearing house for information about industry.
- Training programmes
- awards
- journals.

CLASSIFICATION OF FERTILIZERS

↳ Straight : single compound, one primary nutrient

↳ Compound/complex : single compound, ~~at~~ but two or more primary nutrients in chemically combined form.

↳ Mixture : - physically mixing of two or more fert —

→ can be two or more straight fert

→ . . . straight with complex

→ produced on small scale just before use

→ use prepared to meet specific needs.

Straight —
- Nitrogeneous
- Phosphatic
- Potassic

NITROGENEOUS

→ in form of NH_4^+, NO_3^- (inorganic), $-NH_2$ (amide) and $-CN_2$ (cyanamide) (organic).

↓

readily soluble in H_2O and dissociate spontaneously to release the ions.

→ NO_3^- most of the plants

→ NH_4^+ → rice, tomato etc

$NH_4^+ \longrightarrow NO_3^-$
↳ nitrification

$NH_4^+ \longrightarrow NO_2^-$ (fast process — so no built up of NO_2^-)
↳ Nitrosomonas

$NO_2^- \longrightarrow NO_3^-$
↳ Nitrobacter (biochemical oxidation)

→ NO_3^- → liable to leaching

→ NH_4^+ → retained by –vely charged soil colloids.

→ $-NH_2$ / $-CN_2$ → need to be converted to inorganic.

↳ involves biochemical reactions.

↳ ammonification.

↓ NH_4^+

→ biochemical conversion to nitrate ions.

→ physiochemical reaction with soil colloids

(yields)

SYNTHETIC NITRO. FERT

Three processes —
- cyanamide (crude Ca cyanamide)
- arc (dilute HNO_3 a)
- direct synthetic ammonia (anhy. NH_3)

CALCIUM CYANAMIDE PROCESS 18 quiet – 19 dose.

- developed in Germany (1897–1905) quiet – lagdose
- Prof Dr Adolf Frank and Dr Nicoderm Caro
- ↓ patent in 1900 (lagdod)
- important fert. during World War I.
  - ↳ Reasons → cheap
    - → need lower electrical energy.
    - → used in explosives
    - → easy.

→ not produced in India.

Process

Burning of limestone in a kiln (1100°C)

→ 1100–1300°C (presence of atm N_2)

$$CaCO_3 \xrightarrow{heat} CaO + CO_2$$

↓

$$CaO + 3C \text{ (coal/coke)} \rightarrow CaC_2 + CO$$

(calcium carbide)

$$CaC_2 + N_2 \rightarrow CaCN_2 + C.$$

(calcium cyanamide).

$CaCN_2$ – easily conv to NH_3.

– ~~not~~

ARC PROCESS

- Simplest ✓
- imitating reaction between N_2 and O_2 in the atmosphere. (due to lightning)
- Prof. Christian Birkland and Samuel Eyde (laqdon-door) (1902-04)
- disadvantage: requires large amount of energy. (5 times of $CaCN_2$ process)
  - high capital cost

blowing air in arc → $N_2 + O_2 \xrightarrow[3500°C]{heat} 2NO$ (in an electric arc) nitrous oxide

$2NO + O_2 \longrightarrow 2NO_2$ (nitric oxide)

$2NO_2 + H_2O \longrightarrow 2HNO_3 + NO$.

SYNTHETIC AMMONIA PROCESS

- 1910 - Prof. Fritz Haber (laqload) (first plant of syn. NH_3) in Oppau, Germany
- $N_2 + H_2$
- consumes less power
  - ↳ most popular route
- Technical difficulties of handling inflammable gases at high temperature and ~~gase~~ pressure tackled by Dr Carl Bosch (1913)

→ Thus, Haber-Bosch process.

→ needs two gases N_2 and H_2 → $N_2 + H_2$ → producer gas

N_2: Obtained from atm air by fractional distillation of liquefied air
or → blowing air over burning coal when O_2 of the air combines with C of coal to form CO/CO_2 leaving N_2 unchanged

source of H_2
↳ called feedstock. (natural gas to/complex naptha/heavy fuel oil).
or electrolysis of H_2O
or water gas
coke oven gas
refinery gas.

Extraction of H_2 from these feedstocks involves:-

- desulphurization - removing S (that poisons the catalyst)
- Primary reformation
  (1300°C, high pressure, in presence of Ni-catalyst
  - ↳ Breaks down hydrocarbons
  - ↳ releasing C as CO/CO_2 and H_2 gas.
- Secondary ref.
  $CO \rightarrow CO_2$ in presence of Ni-catalyst
- Shift converter, using Fe_2O_3 and Cr_2O_3 catalyst
  remaining traces of $CO - CO_2$
  $CO + H_2O \rightarrow$ release H_2
  $CO_2 + H_2O \rightarrow$ release H_2 }
- CO_2 absorber → CO_2 is finally removed.

$$3H_2 + N_2 \rightleftharpoons 2NH_3$$

400-450°C; Fe_2O_3 (catalyst) / Al_2O_3, K_2O, Mg, CaO (promoter); 200-1000 kg cm^{-2} (elevated pressure); birth

- → exothermic (647 Kcal/kg of NH_3)
- → using Fe-catalyst promoted with Al, K.
- → Gas mixture of $N_2 : H_2$ of 1:3 plus 10%-14% inerts (mainly CH_4, Ar and He) and 2% NH_3 is used.

(3:1)

STORAGE OF NH_3

- → at atm pressure if it is cooled to -33°C 'or'
- → stored under high pressure
- Anhy. NH_3 - most concentrated form (82% N).
- → can be stored as a liquid — fully refrigerated / semi / pressurized condition

PRODUCTION OF NITROGENOUS FERTILISERS

i) Ammonium Sulphate (CRH—81)

- low analysis fert — How many sulphur?
- 20.6% N. (need .d) — ↳ 23.7% S.
- must not mixed with lime.
- Processes:—

i) $2NH_3 + H_2SO_4 \rightarrow (NH_4)_2SO_4$. — byproduct of steel ind.

or ii) scrubbing coke oven-gas with H_2SO_4.

or iii) $(NH_4)_2CO_3 + CaSO_4 \rightarrow (NH_4)_2SO_4 + CaCO_3$

↳ $CaCO_3$: filtration; $(NH_4)_2SO_4$: evaporation and crystallization.

Gypsum process

→ Caprolactum process – interm. prod. of synth. fibre industry.

or iv) gaseous $NH_3 + H_2SO_4$ in spray tower – Gujarat State Fert Corp. – 1974

or v) NH_3 + mixed acid → $(NH_4)_2SO_4$ and other amm. salts

ii) Ammonium chloride

- 25% N (nose)
- Dual Salt Process
- known as Solvay Process
- Produce both NH_4Cl and $NaHCO_3/NaCO_3$.
- In solvay plants

↳ ammoniated solution of 30% NaCl is treated with CO_2 to form $(NH_4)_2CO_3$.

$$2NH_3 + H_2O + CO_2 \rightarrow (NH_4)_2CO_3$$

More addition of carbon dioxide produces NH_4HCO_3.

$$(NH_4)_2CO_3 + H_2O + CO_2 \rightarrow 2NH_4HCO_3$$

Addition of NaCl.

$$NH_4 \cdot HCO_3 + NaCl \rightarrow NaHCO_3 + NH_4Cl.$$

↳ $NaHCO_3$ calcined to get $NaCO_3 + CO_2$

NH_4Cl: liquour is ammonated and salted out by addn of NaCl → washed → precipitate → Centrifuse → Dried

- Direct neutralization Process

$NH_{3(g)} + HCl_{(l)} \rightarrow NH_4Cl$.

neutralization of NH_3 by HCl.

- Ammonium nitrate mixed with $CaCO_3$ to produce CAN ($NH_4NO_3 + CaCO_3$) – neutral fert

↓

Kisan Khad (farmer's fert)

↓

25% N < equal NH_3 / eq. NO_3^-

$CaCO_3$ – lowers hazardous effect

NITRIC ACID

- 800 -1000°C
- In presence of platinum and rhodium catalyst
- continuous oxidation

$4NH_3 + 5O_2 \rightarrow 4NO + 6H_2O$ = – 54.14 kcal/gmol.

$2NO + O_2 \rightarrow 2NO_2$ = –13.6

$4NO_2 + O_2 + 2H_2O \rightarrow 4HNO_3$ = 20.8.

See arc process

AMMONIUM NITRATE

- 35% N (ms)
- But risk of fire
- So mixed with limestone as CAN. (26% N) (nib)
- Several processes – combinations of neutralization, evaporation, drying, finishing.

// neutralization

$NH_3 + HNO_3 \rightarrow NH_4NO_3$ (80% concn.)

// CAN:– concent. $NH_4NO_3 + CaCO_3 \rightarrow$ CAN. (granulated) + a clay conditioner (surface coating) to improve physical prop. of CAN.

SOIL SCIENCE SOIL SCIENCE

UREA

- 1773 identified after isolation in crystalline form from urine
- first organic compound synthesised from inorganic materials

$2NH_3 + CO_2 \rightleftharpoons NH_2CO_2NH_4$. (exothermic 37.7 kcal/g mol) meet.t − t.t

$NH_4CO_2NH_4 \rightleftharpoons CO(NH_2)_2 + H_2O$ (endo −7.7 kcal/g mol)

- contains 45-46% N.
- methods for production — once through partial recycle / total recycle process.

Once through partial recycle

liquid NH_3 and CO_2 gas → introduced → urea reactor at 185°C at 200 atmosphere → 35% NH_3 and 75% CO_2 converted to urea.

effluents (contain 80% urea)

Unconverted NH_3 and CO_2

→ a portion of it is recycled

Total → whole − 99% recovery.

- Urea marketed in form of prills in India though other forms are granules, flake, crystal.
- Molten urea is prilled by spraying over a prill tower
  - droplets - cooled
- To improve physical strength and resistance to caking -
  - fomaldehyde (0.3% − 0.4%)
  - or talc, powdery mat, china clay
  - medium viscosity oil (without clay) → to reduce moisture absorp.

- Biuret
  - $NH_2-CO-NH-CO-NH_2$
  - limit 2%
  - damage to foliage
  - citrus more sensitive.

PHOSPHATIC

Raw materials → Phosphatic rock, H_2SO_4.

SULPHORIC ACID

- 60% of world's H_2SO_4 prodn based on → Elemental S
  25% . . . → Pyrites.

Elemental sulfur → (burnt in dry air 950-1100°C) SO_2 → SO_3
↓ absorbed in dilute H_2SO_4
↳ 98% concentration H_2SO_4.

- Principal processes for conversion of SO_2 to SO_3
  → Chamber process
  → contact process (more common) with a metal/metal oxide (Vanadium oxide) as catalyst.

PHOSPHATIC ROCK (main)

- any rock — large proportion of phosphatic minerals
- Produced by mining and beneficiation
- Minerals of 2 groups → apatite; aluminuous phosphate
- 32% P_2O_5 content (w/w)
- Produced mainly by USA, China, Morocco, Russia
- Apatites occur in ign. meta. sedi.
  → most imp ones yielding large proportion of Ca-phosphates
  commercial - fluorapatite $Ca_{10}(PO_4)_6F_2$
  chief source of P.

Aluminuous phosphate → Crandalite, Wavellite, Millisite

APATITES

- Basically calcium phosphates
- $Ca_{10}(PO_4)_6F_2$ → primary source of P.
- occurs in igneous, metamorphic and sedime
  large yield
- carbonate substituted apatite
  ↳ francolite or carbonate apatite.

$$Ca_{10-a-b}Na_a Mg_b (PO_4)_{6-x}(CO_3)_x F_{0.4x} F_2$$

a → molar substitution of Na for Ca

b → . . . . Mg for Ca.

x → . . . . CO_3 & F for PO_4.

x = 0 - 1.2.

PHOSPHORIC ACID

- end product (to a less extent)
- intermediate product for a phosphatic fertilizer industry.
- contributes to 90% of P produced
- Processes — Furnace Processes / Wet Processes.

FURNACE PROCESS

$$Ca_{10}(PO_4)_6F_2 + 15C + 6SiO_2 \xrightarrow{furnace} 1.5P_4 + 15CO + 3(3CaO.2.SiO_2) + CaF_2$$

Phosphate rock; Coke; (silica)

$$P_4 + SO_2 \longrightarrow 2P_2O_5$$

$$P_2O_5 + 3H_2O \longrightarrow 2H_3PO_4$$

- Thermal grade acid → highly pure but expensive.

WET PROCESS

$$Ca_{10}(PO_4)_6F_2 + 10H_2SO_4 + 10nH_2O \rightarrow 10CaSO_4.nH_2O + 6H_3PO_4 + 2HF$$

PHOSPHATES

SINGLE SUPERPHOSPHATE (SSP)

- first fertilizer to be produced industrially - 1843 - England
- normal superphosphate
- advantages
  - → production process simple
  - → provides Ca and S besides P
  - → effectiveness unquestioned
  - → ~~Econo~~ small plants viable
  - → not capital intensive → plan operate on a planned seasonal schedule.

→ disadvantage
- low analysis (16-22% P_2O_5)
- high distribution and application costs per unit of P_2O_5 as compared to high analysis

Production process of SSP

- Mixing with powdered phosphate rock (30-38 % P_2O_5) with H_2SO_4 (65 – 75% H_2SO_4) to → slurry

↓

Sot Denning
(solidification of the slurry in den)
crystallization of monocalcium phosphate 0.5 -4 hours

↓

final curing (2-6 weeks)

↓

Dried material crushed into coarse powder

↓

If granular is desired — granulated before or after curing.

Overall :—

$$Ca_{10}(PO_4)_6F_2 + 7H_2SO_4 + 3H_2O \rightarrow 3Ca(H_2PO_4)_2 H_2O + 7CaSO_4 + 2HF$$

Overall reaction in two stages:—

Apatite + H_2SO_4 → H_3PO_4. (rapid)

H_3PO_4 + remaining apatite → monocalcium phosphate (slow)

SSP → mixture of gypsum and water soluble monocalcium phosphate.

↓

Reason of low analysis.

ENRICHED SUPERPHOSPHATE

- double superphosphate
- mixture of SSP + TSP
- apatite + mixed acid ($H_2SO_4 + H_3PO_4$). mis-mis
- advantage fairly high P_2O_5 (25–35%) and presence of Ca & S.

FERTILIZERS DERIVED FROM PHOSPHORIC ā

TRIPLE SUPERPHOSPHATE (TSP)

$Ca_{10}(PO_4)_6F_2 + 14H_3PO_4 + 10H_2O \rightarrow 10\,Ca(H_2PO_4)_2 \cdot H_2O + 2HF$

- concentrated   Advantages
- containing water soluble monocalcium phosphate
- a part of it → comes directly → phosphate rock.

Disadvantages

- acidic (destroy bags)
- unsuitable with urea

- 46% of total P_2O_5
- 42.5% water soluble P_2O_5

rob — ran.s

AMMONIUM PHOSPHATES (AP)

- diammonium phosphates (DAP) most popular complex.
- NH_3 + Tribasic H_3PO_4 → ammonium phosphate
- Only mono-calcium phosphates and DAP are produced.
  ↳ (MAP) $H_3PO_4 + NH_3 \rightarrow NH_4H_2PO_4$.
- while TAP is not produced → unstable (decomposes – due to alkalinity
  ↓ release NH_3 → and converts into DAP)

- DAP preferred over MAP
  Reason → 18-46-0 (higher N) ↳ need more N at planting
  → 11-52-0.

- Granular DAP production :—

$2NH_3 + H_3PO_4\ (40\%\ P_2O_5) \rightarrow (NH_4)_2HPO_4$.

(2 : 1)

⇒

AMMONIUM POLYPHOSPHATES (AP)

- superphosphoric (polyphosphoric ā) + NH_3. 69 - 75% P_2O_5
  - ↳ produced by ~~thermal grade ā~~ concentrating H_3PO_4 of (wet process, or absorbing P_2O_5 in less H_2O than needed to get orthophosphoric ā.
- $H_{n+2} P_n O_{3n+1}$
- In am. polyphosp. P (NH_3) → orthophosphate (plant usable form) ; non-orthophosphate need hydrolysis to → orthophosphate

AMMONIUM PHOSPHATE SULPHATE (APS / ASP)

- two salts of NH_3.
- Best known grade 16-20-0.
- consist of MAP & ~~Amm~~ $(NH_4)_2SO_4$.
  - ↓ Presence of SO_4^{2-} – correct deficiency of N, P, S.
- High critical relative humidity 91.6 % at 30°C
  - ↳ good physical prop.
- Reacting ~~sul~~ H_2SO_4, H_3PO_4 + NH_3.

AMMONIUM PHOSPHATE NITRATE (APN)

- ammonium phosphate, NH_4NO_3.
- 25-25-0, 30-10-0. ↳ somewhat hygroscopic
- Mixed H_3PO_4 + HNO_3 → neutralize NH_3.

UREA AMMONIUM PHOSPHATES (UAP)

- Urea + AP
- 28-28-0, 22-22-11

NITROPHOSPHATES

- phosphate rock with nitric ā
  - provides fert. N.
  - converts phos. rock into more soluble

$Ca_{10}(PO_4)_6F_2 + 14HNO_3 \longrightarrow 3Ca(H_2PO_4) + 7Ca(NO_3)_2 + 2HF$

monocalcium phosphate; calcium nitrate → makes hygroscopic (disadvantage)

↳ analogous with SSP production

- 8% N, 16% P_2O_5
- Nitrophosphate processes involve dissolution of phosphate rock in HNO_3 (50-60% HNO_3)

$Ca_{10}(PO_4)_6F_2 + 20HNO_3 \longrightarrow 6H_3PO_4 + 10Ca(NO_3)_2 + 2HF$.

- Removal of $CaNO_3$ → by cooling mother liquour f.b crystallization
  - 'or' — ion exchange (passing ↓ in K-loaded resin)
  - 'or' — ppt of Ca as $CaSO_4$ by addition of soluble SO_4.
  - 'or' Adjusting $CaO : P_2O_5$ ratio by add. of soluble P_2O_5.
- ammoniation f.b
  - ↳ granulated

BASIC SLAG

- Thomas slag
- byproduct of steel industry
- 10-20% P_2O_5
- But in India (2-5% P_2O_5)
- mainly as Ca-silicophosphate (insoluble in H_2O)
  (fraction soluble in 2% citric ā).
  ↳ potentially plant avail.

POTASSIUM PHOSPHATES

- excellent H_2O soluble
- mono potassium dihydrogen phosphate (KH_2PO_4)
- 0-52-35 ↗ ~~0-~~ 0 - ~~m~~ sin - mis
- di~~ng~~potassium hydrogen phosphate (K_2HPO_4)
  0-40-54 ↗ 0 - vide - sir
- tetrapotassium pyrophosphate ($K_4P_2O_7$)
  0-43-57 ↗ 0 - room - sit
- Potassium metaphosphate (KPO_3)
  0 - bad - ~~s~~ rod
  0-60-40 ↗
- KOH / ~~K~~ CO_3 + H_3PO_4 ⟶ ~~

BONE MEAL

- good source of P in acid soils and its slow solubility has a long term effect
- expensive.
- used in animal feeds.

FUSED CALCIUM MAGNESIUM SO_4

- fusing $Ca_{10}(PO_4)_6F_2$ + olivine / serpentine (Mg silicate) in an electric furnace.
- glass-like
- 20% P_2O_5 - 15% MgO
- 90% P → citric acid soluble.

DEFLUORINATED PHOSPHATE ROCK

- ~~ha~~ High grade P.R + small amt $NaCO_3$ / Na_2SO_4 + H_3PO_4.
- calcined at 1350°C
- 38-42% P_2O_5 (90% citric & 2%)

mug jin

RHENANIA PHOSPHATE nag-mud

- P.R + Na_2CO_3 + Silica → calcined - kiln - 1250°C.
- 28 - 30% P_2O_5 (neutral or alk. NH_4 citrate soln soluble).

DICALCIUM PHOSPHATE

- common constituent of nitrophosphates, ammoniated SSP.
- P.R + HCl → ppt as dica-phosphate by adn of limestone.

DIRECT APPLn OF P.R

- old practice
- contributn to total P consumptn → marginal.
- ~~may not exceed 50%~~ of ze
- varies with soil charac.

POTASH FERTILIZERS

- mined first in 1861.
- Canada, Russia → ½ of world reserve.
- K-bearing minerals :- sylvite, langbeinite, kainite, carnallite.
- most mined ore: sylvinite (sylvite + halite)
  - sylvite ↓ KCl, halite ↓ NaCl

POTASSIUM CHLORIDE (KCl)

- Extracted from underground deposits of sylvinite.
- Shaft mining (depth < 1300), solution mining (>1300 m), from brines (sea).
- ↓
  Benefication → Dried → Marketed as KCl.
  (removes impurities, NaCl)
  → solution crystallization
  → Heavy media separation
  → Froth floatation
  ↳ common
  floating off crystals of KCl or NaCl and harvest.

K_2SO_4

- $KCl + H_2SO_4 \longrightarrow KHSO_4 + HCl$ (exo)

$KHSO_4 + KCl \longrightarrow K_2SO_4 + HCl$ (endo)

or'

$4KCl + 2SO_2 + O_2 + 2H_2O \longrightarrow 2K_2SO_4 + 4HCl.$
(hot SO_2)

$CaSO_4 . 2H_2O$ — 16

FeS.

SSP

$Ca(H_2PO_4) + Ca$

SULPHUR SOURCES	FORMULA	SULPHUR CONTENT (%)
SSP	$Ca(H_2PO_4) + CaSO_4 \cdot 2H_2O$	12-14
Ammonium sulphate	$(NH_4)_2SO_4$	24
Ammonium phosphate sulphate	$(NH_4)_2SO_4 + (NH_4)_2HPO_4$.	13
Potassium sulphate	K_2SO_4	18
Gypsum	$CaSO_4 \cdot 2H_2O$	16
Pyrites	FeS_2	20

MICRONUTRIENT SOURCES	FORMULA	CONTENT (%)
Zinc sulphate, heptahydrate	$ZnSO_4 \cdot 7H_2O$	21. (Zn) — nil
- - - - monohydrate	$ZnSO_4 \cdot H_2O$	33 (Zn) — mam
Manganese sulphate	$MnSO_4 \cdot H_2O$	30.5 (Mn) — mob.s
Ferrous sulphate	$FeSO_4 \cdot 7H_2O$	19 (Fe) — laq
Copper sulphate	$CuSO_4 \cdot 5H_2O$	24 (Cu) — nory
Sodium borate (Borax)	$Na_2B_4O_7 \cdot 10H_2O$	10.5 (B)
Ammonium molybdate	$(NH_4)_6Mo_7O_{24} \cdot 2H_2O$	52 (Mo). — Sin

SECONDARY NUTRIENTS

- In India, ~~only~~ principal source - elemental sulphur
  ↳ imported
- also exists in atmosphere as SO_2 ↓ falls with snow and rainfall.
- contributes 3-30 kg of S/ha/yr.

MIXED FERTILIZERS

FERTILIZER GRADE

- guaranteed minimum percentage of N, P_2O_5, K_2O
- separated by hyphens.

FERT. RATIO

- ratio of the percentages of N, P_2O_5, K_2O.

CONDITIONERS AND FILLERS

↓

materials added during prepartⁿ to ↓ hygroscopicity and ↑ physical condition

↳ low grade organic materials.

Filler : wt make up material added to get fert-grade of desired.

eg. sand, soil, coal powder, china clay.

TYPES OF FERTILIZER MIXTURES

Open formula : kinds and qualities of ingredients disclosed

closed formula : not disclosed

↳ disadvantage to the farmers cannot know the kind and quality of the nutrients.

MATERIALS USED IN FERTILIZER MIXTURES

- Suppliers of plant nutrients
- conditioners : good drilling condⁿ, reduce caking
  100 kg/tonne
  tobacco stems, paddy husk, groundnut shell
- Neutralizers of Residual acidity.
  acidic - $(NH_4)_2SO_4$ or $CO(NH_2)_2$
  added dolomitic limestone.
- Filler.

INCOMPATIBILITIES IN FERTILIZER MIXTURES

- comprehend - have good knowledge.

i) containing NH_3 → should not mixed with basically reactive fertilizers → loss of N →

ii) no water soluble phosphate (SSP, TSP and $(NH_4)_2HPO_4$) mixed with those cont. free lime

↳ make it insoluble

iii) easily soluble and hygroscopic (CAN, NH_4NO_3, urea) → caking → mixed just before use

iv) slightly acidic SSP → liberate acid → damage gunny bags and drilling implements.

Bonemeal - used as a drier in mixing.

METHODS OF MIXING

- Farm-mixed - economical - on cement floor - spade, a hammer, wee
  ↳ mixed on day of appln or a day before (avoid caking)
  If not immediately used
  ↳ mix filler.
- factory-made
  ↳ Types
  → Dry-mix plant (all str fert mixed in dry form)
  → plant in which NH_3 added to P and K fert.

→ SSP manufactured from $Ca_{10}(PO_4)_6F_2$ and H_2SO_4 and
↳ is utilized for prep.

→ manufacture their own reqd of H_2SO_4 to prepare SSP.

GRANULATED FERTILISER MIXTURES

- high analysis
-

SOIL ORGANIC MATTER ✓

[ISSS]

- intrinsic, ubiquitous.
- FUNCTIONS OF SOM
- food source for microflora, soil fauna / MOs.
- nutrient storehouse of N..
  inorganic N → less available
  so conversion of organic N.
- storehouse of P, S.
- improves chemical properties of soil
  - enhance CEC
  - enhance ligancy in trapping nutrient cations
  - buffering capacity
- improves physical properties
  - soil structure
  - infiltrability
  - porosity
  - soil drainage
- release of nutrients from minerals by weathering
- ~~involves~~ influences soil proccesses → soil formation
- organic materials influence growth and development
- soil health and quality (prime decider)
- NATURE AND AMOUNT OF SOIL ORGANIC MATTER ✓
- litter layer: dead plants residues
  uppermost layer
- partly decomposed plant residues
  : due to action of soil fauna and m/os
- Biological organic molecules: components of plants and animal tissues.
  ↳ non-humic substances
- Humic substances.

- Humic substances – stable end products of decomposition

-> Since agricultural soils contain little litter and decomposed litter layers.

SOM -> non humic substances (10-15% of Total organic mat in soils)

-> humic substances (85-90%)

-> Soil microbial biomass: living pool of SOM excluding plant roots and larger soil fauna (>5×10³ μm)

↳ genetically and functionally diverse

-> soil biomass: flux of energy and interaction among the components

FACTORS OF SOM ACCUMULATION

5-10%

- Cultivation – cultivated soils in temperate regions have high OM levels (5-10%) as compared to that in tropics (1/5th or 1/6th ie < 1%)

< 1%

Organic matter = f (climate, vegetation, time, parent material, topography)

(5)

CLIMATE

- Temperature: SOM decrease 2-3 times for every 10°C rise in mean temperature

↳ decomposition rate more rapid / loss to CO_2

Therefore warmer climate less SOM.

But upto 35°C because above this temperature, suppression of microbial activity.

- Moisture: 60-80% of maximum water holding capacity increases with increase in soil moisture

Tropical evergreen forests rich in om than grassland cover
↳ inputs of litter is much larger.

—within a particular climate.

SOIL MINERALS AND TEXTURE

- soil rich in montmorillonite favour som accumulation
- loamy soils - accumulate SOM.

TOPOGRAPHY

- depressions and valleys - more som.

→ Turnover period of som is about (150) years.

→ Functional pools of som

↳ decomposable
- metabolic litter (plant & an. residues like cellulose. 1-6 months)
- structural litter (plant residues eg. lignin) 3 months - 2 year.

↳ resistant
- ↳ active pool (labile fraction) - 2 months - 1.5 yr viz microbial biomass
- ↳ slow pool (labile viz particulate om) - 8-50 yrs.
- ↳ passive pool (humus) - upto 2000 yrs.

- Quasi-equilibrium values (1-2%)
↳ values reach after a significant reduction of som.

HUMIC SUBSTANCES

- most largest fraction of soil OM
- colloidal, polymeric, dark colours (brown-black and black to yellow)
- Three fractions
  - fulvic acid — soluble in H_2O, acid, alkali (yellow to brownish yellow)
  - humic acid — soluble only in alkalis (dark brown to black)
  - Humin (most insoluble) ↳ attached with soil matrix bounded tightly

CHEMICAL NATURE OF HUMIC SUBSTANCES

- polymeric compounds - built with aromatic units. (mainly)
- The major units → phenols, quinones, aromatic carboxylic acid ~~as~~ with nitrogeneous compounds forming long chain linked by –O–, –NH–, =N–, –(CH_2)– etc bridges.
- aliphatic ~~ure~~ structures (fatty acids) – present as branches.
- ~~A~~ Some of the units –
  - mono, di-, tri- hydroxybenzene
  - benzene carboxylic acid.
  - aromatic nitrogeneous compounds
  - amino a
  - aromatic amines.
  - fatty acids
  - carbohydrates
- Major functional units : phenolic hydroxyl, carboxyl, keton~~e~~ quinone, amine.
- not having a single repeating unit so no single structural formula

carbon - sim - sag rod - sod
Humic acid O_2 - man - mag Fulvic acid mag - rag

- higher carbon but less oxygen —
- less acidic (aromatic) 500 - 900 and hydrophobic 560 - 890 — more acidic (700 - 1400 cmol/kg) hydrophilic — 640 - 1420 — 520 - 1120
- m/w 10,000 - 200,000 — 150 - 570 — few hundreds to thousands
- more polymerized — less.
- longer chain — shorter
- more phenolic -OH — more carboxylic.

In solution
↳ interconversion of FA → HA or HA → FA occurs

~~cleavage of HA molecule~~ undergo reaction to form larger HA (yellow to black)

cleavage of HA molecule. (black → yellow).

- TEM (Transmission electron microscopy)
↳ size of humic mol. → ~~60 x~~ 60 - 100 A^0 ($0.6 - 1.0 \times 10^{-10}$ m)

— globular sphere ↘ coalesce to form network, fibre like structures.

E_4/E_6 ratio of
HA → 3 - 5
FA → 6 - 9.

→ Coiling of humic substances.
↳ because highly flexible
at high dilution/alkaline → uncoiled (-ve charged groups on the macromolecule repel)
at high concentration/salt/acids - coiled -

EXTRACTION OF HUMIC SUBSTANCES FROM SOILS

- occurs in association with clay, minerals, cations.
- involves breakage of such bonds.
- extracted solution is again purified.
- common treatment : with alkali : dilute NaOH / Na_2CO_3
- Converts polyvalent cation humates (insoluble) / mineral humates
  ↓
  · sodium humates

$$Ca\text{-}HA\ /\ clay\text{-}Al\text{-}HA + 2NaOH \rightarrow Na_2\text{-}HA + Ca(OH)_2\ /\ clay\text{-}Al\text{-}(OH)_2$$

- If soil rich in Ca^{2+} → pretreament with dilute HCL
  (to avoid reprecipitation as Calcium humate)

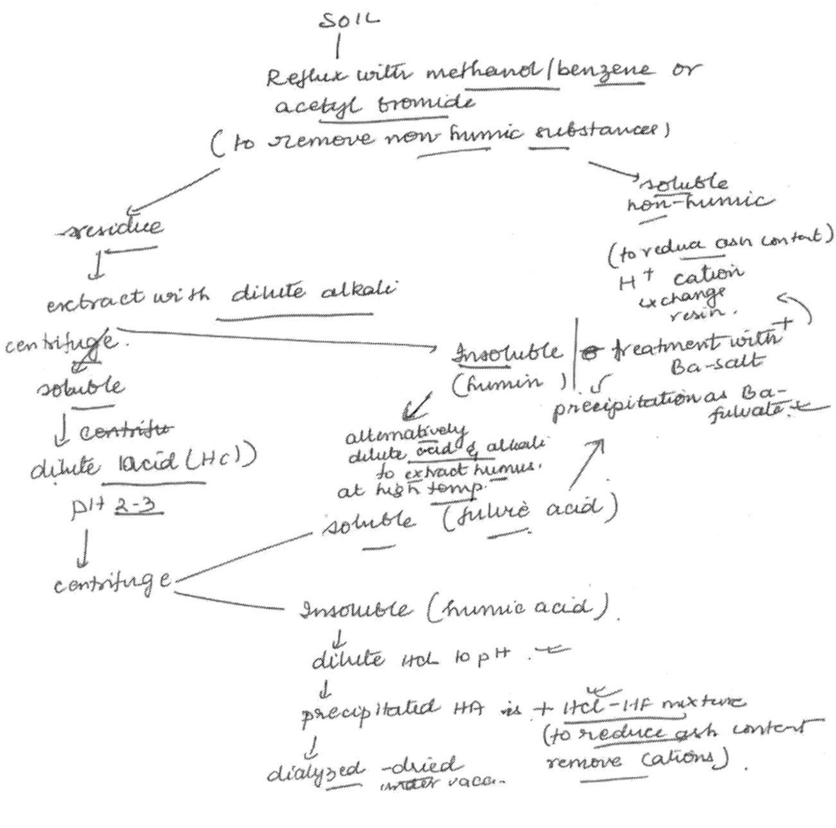

Experimental methods

Elemental analysis

C → combustion ✓
H → combustion ✓
N → Kjeldahl ✓
S → Zeisel methods ✓

Total acidity

- Both FA and HA – weak acid behaviour due to presence of carboxyl and phenolic hydroxyl
- $Ba(OH)_2$ titration in non-aqueous medium under an inert atmosphere ie N_2.

Molecular weight

- viscometer (viscosity measurements)
- using flow of water and viscous at constant temp.
- ↑ the molecular weight → more viscous. time of flow more.

Functional groups and structure

- Spectroscopic methods. study chemical nature of humic substances.
  ↓
  interaction between electromagnetic waves with molecules depends on molecular parameters

- IR spectroscopy ✓
  ↳ absorption of IR radiation by molecules due to vibrations of their func. groups.

  Ex –COOH in HA shows absorption at 1720 cm^{-1} ✓
  –carboxylate ion . . . . 1590 cm^{-1}. ✓

- qualitative measure

Vandmo aals radius of H = 1.2 A°
O = 1.4 A°

[SOIL WATER
PROPERTIES AND BEHAVIOUR]

MOLECULAR STRUCTURE OF WATER

O.quote

- chemical formula H_2O < two H, one O — covalent bonded /
  - H – O → distance 0.97 Å
  - H – H — 1.54 Å – lesser.
- not symmetrical arrangement
- H^+ atoms attached with O^- in an angle of 103–106° (avg 105°) (104.5°)
- asymmetrical arrangements — unequal distribution of charges
- reason of being dipolar / polar
- O → excess negative charge, H^+ – +ve charge
- hydrogen atoms linked with O^- of neighbouring molecule
- called hydrogen bond
- form a cluster of water molecules
- That's why called as polymer of hydrogen bonded molecules.
- space occupied by a H_2O mol - depends on O^{--} ion.
- 2.64 A° nibir re
- 1 cm³ of liquid water contains 3.346×10^{22} molecules

$$\left(\frac{6.023}{18} \times 10^{23} = 3.346 \times 10^{22}\right)$$

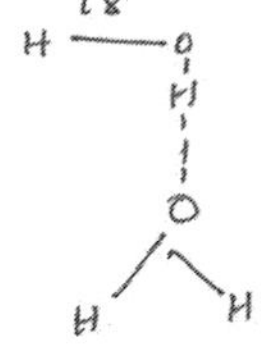

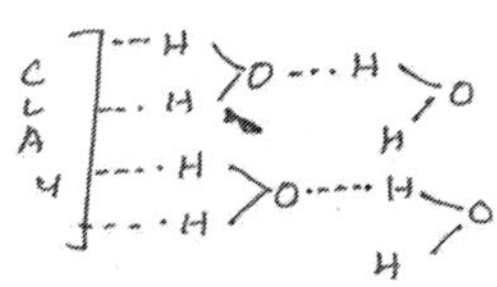

- spherical in shape.

STRUCTURE OF LIQUID WATER AND ICE

- H_2O polymer of hydrogen bonded molecules
- In ice, hydrogen bonding complete
  - ↳ one water molecules bonded with 4 neighbouring H_2O molecules. → open hexagonal layer lattice
- In ~~ice water~~. melting of ice — rigid structure Partially broken —

- additional H_2O molecules enters intermolecular space – each H_2O molecule bonded with more than 4 neighbouring molecules
- Reason of being H_2O denser than ice at same temperature and ice floats in water
- liquid H_2O more potential energy
  - ↳ absorbs 80 cal/gm of heat energy
  - (solid → liquid)
- ice (rigid and permanent structure)
- H_2O (flexible and transitory)
- Flickering cluster model

  hydrogen bonded water microcrystals embeded in a matrix of non hydrogen bonded molecules / free water molecules.
- hydrogen bond: formation – chain
  - breakage – create short lived cluster of highly H-bonded
- H-bond so strong that M.P, B.P, dielectric constant, surface tension, viscosity and specific heat ↑ as compared to others with same molecular weight.
- Soil water adsorbed on surface of soil – more like ice.
  - ↳ less mobility
- kinetic energy min^m in ice, increases in liquid and more in gas forms.
- degree of H-bonding varies with temp and state.

  0°C → 100%

  liquid – 85%

  ↳ 40°C → 50%

  100°C gas → 10%.

SOIL ACIDITY

PROPERTIES OF WATER

DENSITY

- low density due to the open structure of H_2O molecules
- maxm density at ~~40~~ 4°C (1.0 Mg/m³).

4°C upto 50°C
0.988 Mg/m³ (due to more kinetic motion → more space)
↑ temp increases
4°C
↓
0.99 Mg/m³ upto ~~50~~°C (due to hexagonal arrangement more space)

negligible change → so taken generally as 1 Mg/m³

- density between ice and H_2O different → 0.917 Mg/m³ → hydrogen bonding complete
- As ice melts → density increases ~~up~~ to about 9%

In soil surface, water acts like ice so, density is 0.97-0.98 Mg/m³.

Ice like structure extends upto 60 Å from the soil surface.

SURFACE TENSION

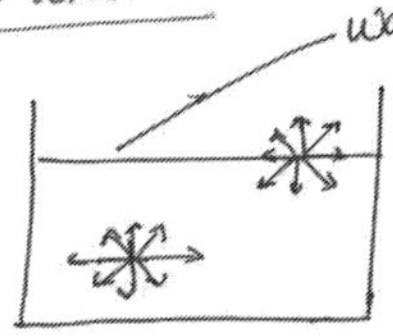

- H_2O molecules inside the liquid attracted in all direction with equal cohesive force.
- but at the interface, more attraction towards the liquid side due to more no. of molecules per unit volume

(tension of the surface film of a liquid caused by attraction of the particles in surface layer by bulk of liquid → ↓ surface area

- Due to this unequal attraction
  - ↳ H_2O tends to contract - minimum surface area → Reason for being spherical
- work must be done to bring the molecules from the bulk of liquid to the surface against inward force → free surface energy
- creates tension → surface tension
  - ↓
  - a force in dynes acting at ~~rt~~ angle to any line of 1 cm length in surface.
  - ergs/cm² = dynes/cm. or dynes/cm² = ergs/cm³
    - ↓ energy/area ↓ force/distance.
- dimension $[M/T^2] = [MT^{-2}]$
- surface tension 72.7 dynes/cm at 20°C.
  - ↓ high due to H-bonding.

Temperature and electrolytes addition

↓

↑ increase → decrease in density due to thermal expansion

↓ reduce cohesive force at surface as well as liquid.

↓ decrease linearly (S.T.)

→ ↑ increase

↓ ~~decrease~~ ↑ increase

more affinity of solute mol. than of H_2O molecules to each other → solutes drawn towards liquid

1.0% increase electrolyte → ↑ 0.17 dynes/cm S.T.

But detergents (organic solutes) decrease S.T.

↳ more cohesive force between H_2O molecules than ~~solute~~ attraction to solute

↓ tends to acc. in surface.

– S.T of soap solution is 80 dynes/cm at 20°C

CONTACT ANGLE OF WATER ON SOLID SURFACE

- angle between the interface of air, ~~and~~ water ~~gas~~ and solid represented by S.T.

- ~~cos θ~~ $\gamma_{GS} = \gamma_{LS} + \gamma_{GL} \cos\theta$ — quantifies the wettability of a solid surface by a liquid via the Young Equation

$\Leftarrow\Rightarrow \cos\theta = \frac{\gamma_{GS} - \gamma_{LS}}{\gamma_{GL}}$ — goniometer

→ If $\gamma_{GS} > \gamma_{LS}$ = $\cos\theta$ = +ve ⇒ θ < 90°

⇒ If $\gamma_{GS} < \gamma_{LS}$ = $\cos\theta$ = −ve ⇒ θ = 90°–180°.

→ ~~when~~ adhesive forces between S and L > cohesive force between H_2O mol. and forces between G and S.

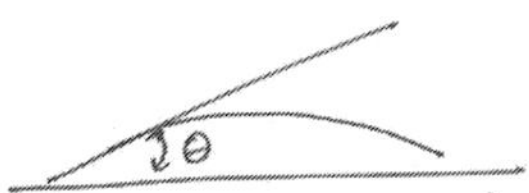

↳ acute θ < 90°

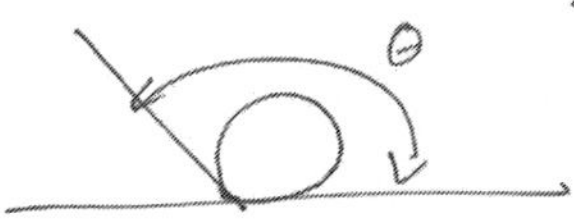

↳ wetting the solid eg. water on glass.

θ = liquid mol. strongly ~~aff~~ attracted to solid ~~surfaces~~ molecules ↓ liquid drop will completely spread out on the solid surface.

→ θ = 90°–180° — not to wet the solid eg. mercury on glass.

– θ = 90 180° → complete nonwetting.

. θ = 0° = complete flattening of water drop = perfect wetting

– Contact angle of advancing angle > c. receding angle

↳ due to surface roughness, adsorbed pressure and distribn of impurities on solid mechanisms of water mole. adsorbed or desorbed.

θ < 90° = solid surface = hydrophillic

> 90° = hydrophobic = many polymers.

Contd/-

[SOIL ORGANIC MATTER]

- UV and visible absorption spectroscopy measures absorption of UV-visible light by HA/FA solutions.
  - ↳ quantitative analysis. ✓

E4/E6 → optical density of HA/FA solutions at 465 nm and 665nm respectively.

FA → have high E4/E6 ✓
→ ~~hum~~

E4/E6 – inverse index of particle size and aromaticity.

→ Fluorescence
  - ↳ characterized by a band at 465 nm in their fluorescence (excitation) spectra

→ NMR (Nuclear Magnetic Resonance)
  - ↳ absorption of radiowaves by atomic nucleus in a strong magnetic field. ↳ long wavelength.
  - ↳ only atoms with odd no. of nucleons (total no. of neutrons and protons)

Strong magnetic field

→ ESR (Electron spin resonance)
  - used to probe both the nature of spins and spin concentrations.

→ Crystallinity
  - XRD – X-ray diffraction.

→ Morphology
  - SEM (Scanning electron microscopy) ✓
    - ↳ higher magnifications.

REACTIONS OF HUMIC SUBSTANCES WITH METAL IONS

- humic substances - several reactive functional groups → make soil efficient soil complexants for transitional ~~or~~ metal ions like Zn^{2+}, Cu^{2+} ..
- functional groups involved in complexation
  - ↳ –OH, $-NH_2$, –COO–, >CO etc
- Two kinds of bonding :–

a) coordinate bonding

functional groups donate a pair of e^- to the vacant orbital in the transitional metal ion.

eg. H_2N-Cu. NH_2-Cu

b) Electrovalent linkage

–ve group bonds with the +vely ~~ch~~ cation

eg. $COO^- Zn^{2+} COO^-$

- Either one or both types of linkages.

Stability of the metal-HA complexes

Cunico
Zincfeman

$Cu^{2+} > Ni^{2+} > Co^{2+} > Zn^{2+} > Fe^{2+} > Mn^{2+}$.

- maximum amt of metal ion that can be bound by humic → depends on total acidic group content
- → metal ions bound to humic sub → recovered by treatment with a strong cation exchange resin.
- plant roots as ion exchangers.

Importance of metal-humic ~~so~~ complex.

- carriers of trace elements
- weathering
- release of micronutrients from primary minerals and insoluble precipitates
- reduces precipitation and leaching loss.
- reduce toxicity of pollutant metal ions (Pb or Cd eg)

[REACTIONS OF HUMIC SUBSTANCES WITH CLAY MINERALS]

- retards soil microbial decomposition of humus.
- same functional groups.
- clay minerals — contains cations at basal and edges to which acidic groups of HA can bond.
- et coordinate bonding and electrovalent linkage also physical bonding.
- In chemical bonding → ~~clay and~~ metal ion forms a bridge. (Clay - Ca^{2+} - HA.)
- Montmorillonite : bonding at basal surface

  Illite : both basal and edges.

  Kaolinite : edges.
- also with sesquioxide.
- Bonding of HA with Fe_2O_3 > HA - FeOOH

FORMATION OF HUMUS IN THE ENVIRONMENT

- Broken down /chemically altered by m/os. and recombined under the influence of enzymes.
- microbes exude extracellular enzymes to break down macromolecules to smaller units

- ~~to~~ These – taken as food by m/o
  a part oxidized to CO_2
  rest – excuded in form of different waste products.

when Lignin is utilized – phenolic acids, polyphenols are produced

Proteins → polypeptides, amino acid.

- common molecular wastes: polyphenols and phenolic acids.
  ↓
  not use as food
  ↓
  accumulate in soil.

- Phenolic: unstable in air.
  polymerize by an oxidative process.
  polymerize under influence of certain enzymes (phenol oxidases)

- Then polymerization begins with ~~at~~
  - nitrogenous compounds
  - sugars.

- more polymerized – HA
  less " – FA

- FA / HA availability determined by O_2 availability

- Under anaerobic conditions – phenol oxidation less
  – less polymerized.

- soil fauna:– helpful.

MANAGEMENT OF SOM

Sources of OM

↳ plant tissues – 40–50% C on dry wt ~~basis~~.

↓ on-farm → off-farm

COMPOSTING

- biological decomposition and stabilization of organic materials in wastes
  - ↳ development of thermophilic at temp (55 – 65°C)
  - ↳ minm duration of 3-4 weeks.
- biologically produced heat
  - ↳ sanitization
  - ↳ minimize the odours. and leachates
- Two stages! –
  - Thermophilic (sanitization)
  - mesophilic (decomposition) — complex organic molecules
    - synthesis of humus
    - Bacteria 80% of microbial pop.

easily degradable substances → upto 55-60°C. within 2-7 days.

- Thermotolerant fungi
- Thermophilic bacteria & actinomycetes
- Vermicomposting
  - ↳ passage of soil through earthworms ↳ excreta/castings rich in nitrate and avl P, K. Ca and Mg

OFF-FARM

- Agro industrial wastes
- Municipal wastes.

MANAGEMENT PRACTICES

- maintain C:N ratio lesser than/narrower 30:1.
- requirement of N → include legumes or add Ni
  - ↳ if C:N ratio wider
- Legume grown for 2 months → then incorp.
  - ↳ 75 – 100 kg of N.

- Incorporation — before sowing
  ↳ for enough decomposition and re-mineralization of the microbially immobilized N.
  ↳ 3-4 weeks required

MICROBIOLOGICAL ASPECTS OF ORGANIC MATTER DECOMPOSITION

- decomposition primarily a microbiological process.
- carried out by heterotrophic microflora and microfauna
  ↳ obtains their food / energy and carbon from organic compounds.
- Mesofauna like earthworms also.
- Two stages in decomposition: —

  Initial 2-3 weeks — primary flora
  Later - secondary flora
  ↳ act upon the compounds produced by primary flora or dead cells of them

  ↓ more in numbers and maximum decomposition.

- OM decomposition useful for microflora: —
  a) energy for growth
  b) carbon for formation of cell
  c) nutrients
  d).

Carbon — continuously incorporated into microbial cells
↳ assimilation

Under aerobic 20-40% of substrate assimilated.
Rest → converted to CO_2 or as products eg organic acids, alcohols.

- Fungi – 30-40% carbon
- Aerobic bacteria - 5-10% C
- Anaerobic bacteria - 2-5% C

- an enzymatic process.
- constitutional enzymes — produced irrespective of the substrate
- Inducible enzymes — presence of a specific substrate
- Further, metabolize its substrate outside/inside the cell.

extracellular → decomp. of polysaccharides because microbial cells impenetrable to large poly. molecules.

intracellular → Monosaccharides eg. glucose

- Organic residues — acted first by extracellular then intracellular

- Anaerobic decomposition
- lower than aerobic
- oxidation to CO_2 is less.
- carbon remains as intermediate product
- due to low carbon metabolism, low yield of microbial biomass → produce organic acids, alcohols, methane, H^+. → detrimental to plant roots

- Acetic a, formic a, butyric a, lactic a, succinic a, phenolic a

Free energy efficiency: $\frac{\text{Amt. of energy captured by biolog. system}}{\text{amt. of energy released during decomposition}}$

SOIL PHYSICS
(SOIL WATER)

CAPILLARITY → ability of a liquid to flow ~~of~~ in narrow spaces without assistance of or even in opposition to external forces like gravity.

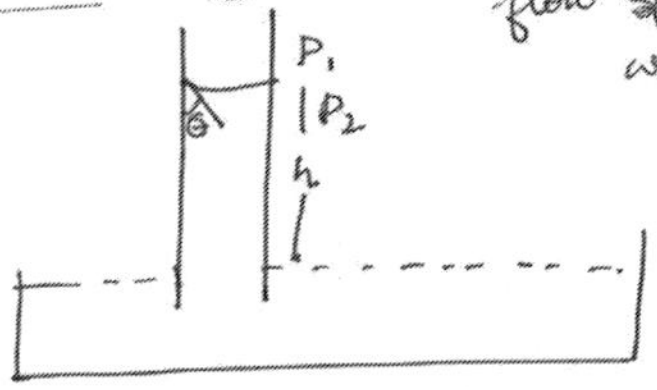

- pressure difference on two sides — depends on radius of curvature
- Pressure below the meniscus < than atmo. pressure.
- pressure below the meniscus → less by $2\gamma/\alpha$

α = radius of curvature.

- narrower the tube, smaller α, larger the pr. diff.
- hydrostatic pressure of h cm column of water

i.e. $hg(\rho_w - \rho_a)$ = pressure diff. ~~between~~ curved meniscus and flat surface

$= 2\gamma/\alpha$.

so, $\alpha = r/\cos\theta$

$$2\gamma/\alpha = hg(\rho_w - \rho_a)$$

$$\Rightarrow 2\frac{\gamma\cos\theta}{r} = hg(\rho_w - \rho_a)$$

$$\Rightarrow h = \frac{2\gamma\cos\theta}{rg(\rho_w - \rho_a)}$$

Then,

$\gamma = 72.7$ dynes/cm $= 72.7 \times 10^{-3}$ N/m²

$\cos\theta = 1$

$g = 9.81$ m/s²

$\rho_w = 1.$ Mg/m³

ρ_a = negl.

$\Rightarrow h = \frac{0.15}{r} = \frac{0.3}{d}$

r = cm.

- height of capillarity
  - ↳ influenced by temp
    - ↳ density and surface tension

ht. of capi - decreases with increasing temp.

↳ depends on largest pore.

Larger the diameter → faster is water rise

So, capillary rise faster in coarse textured.

→ max^m in saturated /wet soil

min^m in dry soil.

↓

due to decrease in water movement in decrease with H_2O content and movement ceases to about 1 atm tension (pF 3)

ATTRACTION OF H_2O TO SOLIDS AND TO INORGANIC IONS

- dipolar
- electrostatic forces.

WATER AS SOLVENT

- Reasons
- dipolar
- high dielectric constant — reduces electric attraction of dissolved ions → so can't combine together
- hydrogen bonding

VISCOSITY

- 20°C - 1 centipoise (1/100th of a poise)
- high viscosity due to hydrogen bonding
- Temp ↑ → viscosity ↓.

→ used in fractionation of soil.

VAPOUR PRESSURE

- pressure excerted by the vapour of a liquid formed at any temperature
- pressure excerted by water vapour which is in equi^{ln} with free and pure H_2O – saturation vapour pressure.
- pres maxm pressure
- due to dipole nature, H_2O vapour pressure low.
- vapour pressure of ice and water at 0°C = same
- " " " boiling water = 1 atmosphere
- v.p ↑ with ↑ temperature due to ↑ thermal motion
- electrolytes/solute → ↓ the vapour pressure due to reduction of partial molar free energy of water.

Related terms

Relative humidity = degree of saturation of the air as aqueous vapour.

Vapour density = mass of H_2O vapour per unit vol. of air

Specific humidity = $\frac{\text{mass of } H_2O \text{ vapour}}{\text{mass of air}}$

Vapour pressure deficit = vapour pressure (existing) – saturation vapour pressure at same temperature

dew point : temp at which mass of air becomes saturated with the quantity of vapour.

vapour pre. of wet and moist soil – nearly 100%

→ ↓ as well as relative humidity → water cont ↓.

Schofield (1935)

pF = ~~log + 2~~ 6.5 + log[2 - R.H]

↓

log of ht of water column (cm) to produce desired suction

FREEZING AND THAWING

- Freezing : → liquid - solid
  Thawing : — solid - liquid.
- Temp solidification occurs : freezing point
  Temp melting occurs : melting point — 0 °C
- Freezing
  ↳ exothermic — heat of freezing
  80 cal/gm.
- freez. point ↓ → presence of solute
  ↓1.85 °C per 1 gm mole of solute in 100 gm of H_2O
- cause : solute molecules interfere in formation of ice like structure
  ↳ freezing point depression
- freezing point ↓ with ↑ pressure
  inhibits the expansion
- of soil water is near to 0°C
  ↳ ↓ decreases with ↓ in H_2O content
- Schofield 1935

$$pF = 4.1 + \log FPD$$

→ Latin word pondus

F = thermodynamic free energy

- Thawing - endothermic
  (80 cal/gm)

VAPOURISATION AND CONDENSATION OF H_2O

Vapourization — evaporation / ebullition / boiling

Evaporation	Ebullition
– slow process	fast
– surface	whole mass
– all temperatures	100 °C

– evaporation : endothermic

a 0°C → 590 cal/gm

latent heat of evaporation

– cooling effect

– Boiling : heat of evaporation at boiling point 537 cal/gm

– Boiling point ↑ with increase in pressure.

– B.P ↓ 1°C ⟶ Pressure ↓ 26.1 mm.

– B.P ↑ ⟶ ↑ salt content

– B.P ↑ 0.52°C ⟶ per gm of solute in 1 litre of H_2O.

– Condensation : exothermic (590 cal/gm).

HEAT OF SUBLIMATION

80 + 590 = 670 gm cal.

HEAT CAPACITY

↳ quantity of heat reqd to raise the temp of a body through 1°C

– Specific heat : 1 gm – 1°C. (of ice : 0.49/0.5 cal/gm)

– H.C of H_2O ↑ → 1 cal/gm. ⟶ 1/2

due to hydrogen bond (of air : 0.17 cal gm.)

– 85

DIELECTRIC CONSTANT

↓

- non-conductor of electricity
- $\varepsilon = \frac{C_w}{C_a}$

C_w = capacitance of an electric condenser in pure H_2O

C_a = - - - - - - - - vacuum/air

Capacitance is the property – to store electrical charge.

= ε = attractive forces between opp. charges . .

= ε ↓ → attraction ↑ and possibility of their combination ↑ → insulate both ions and developing ion.

= pure water ε = 78.5 at 25°C

H_2O molecules are strongly oriented in electric field and less free to move.

IMPORTANCE OF H_2O IN AGRICULTURE

- major part of the plant
- photosynthesis
- turgidity of the plant
- good universal solvent
- carriers of nutrient
- affects soil properties
- microbial activity
- process of weathering
- soil erosion
- soil genesis.

BEHAVIOUR OF H_2O IN SOIL

- hydrogen bonding and surface tension → capillarity ↓ retention of H_2O

↓

H_2O molecules on solid surfaces (adhesion)

- Moisture potentials dry soil pF = above 4.5

tension of water
- Moist soil pF = 4.5 – 2.8
- wet soil pF = ↓ 2.8
- saturated = 0.

RETENTION OF SOIL WATER IN THE FIELD

- in soil pores and surfaces of the solid (colloidal particles)
- surface tension, surface adsorption and capillarity

surface adsorption ↓ depends on colloidal properties

capillarity ↓ radius of soil pores.

- state of soil water in terms of its free energy – potential
- Schofield (1935) – pF

express energy with which the water is held by the soil.

P = logarithm

F = free energy of soil H_2O in terms of an equivalent hydraulic head.

pF advantage: – can plot wide range of moisture conditions on one graph.

– simplify terms.

disadvantage – where only wet range – no purpose

where tension = 0, log 0 = no value

- highest wet condition – saturation

lowest wet condition – air dryness

Maximum retentive capacity

soil H_2O of ~~an undist~~ a disturbed soil sample of 1 cm high & → equil^m with to water table below.

Moisture tension → close to 0 (0.00098 bar

pF = 0)

FIELD CAPACITY

amount of H_2O held after excess H_2O has drained away and the rate of downward movement of water is negligible → within 2-3 days of heavy rain/irrigation.

- tension 1/10th bar (for coarse) pF 2
  1/3rd bar (for ~~light~~ heavy) pF 2.5

WILTING COEFFICIENT (PERMANENT WILTING POINT)

- soil wetness below which the soil H_2O extraction by plants - insufficient to meet ~~evaporat~~transpiration needs
- at which wilted plant fail to recover its turgidity
- 15 bar
- pF 4.2

HYGROSCOPIC COEFFICIENT

- amount of soil H_2O when an air dry soil is kept in an nearly saturated atmosphere (98% RH) until it absorbs no water (equilm with the atmosphere)
- 31 bar tension
- pF 4.5

MOISTURE EQUIVALENT

- % of H_2O held by 1 cm thick soil (saturated) after subjected to a centrifugal force of 1000 times the gravity for 1/2 hour.
  - ME = FC
  - But for sand (ME < FC)

$FC = 0.86\, ME + 2.6\, WC$

$\Rightarrow WC = \frac{ME}{1.84}$.

$FC = 0.gab\, ME + n.ib\, WC$

$WC = \frac{ME}{1.84}$

FACTORS AFFECTING FIELD CAPACITY

FC for sand: 50%
for clayey: 40%
organic soils: more than 100%

Soil texture

increases with increase in fineness but upto SILT LOAM and then remain unchanged or increase slightly

Soil structure

- granular and crumby

Type of clay

expanding

Organic matter content

increases

Soil compaction

decreases

Impeding layers

decreases.

FACTORS – PWP (soil properties + properties of plant) [stage, nature]

Soil texture – increase with clay

Soil structure – not much

clay — expanding

OM content – increase → small

Properties of the plant

rooting density, rooting depth and rate of root extension

- Mesophilic plants – WC → 10–25 bar
  Arid and semi arid → survive even at > 25
  humids and sub humide – < 10.

→ early stages

CONCEPT OF HYGROSCOPICITY

equil^m between the atmosphere and the sample of dry soil
↳ of H_2O vapour

- heat of wetting (heat evolved)
  ↳ due to energy released due to adhesion of H_2O molecules to surface.

- moisture content at which no hygroscopicity

FACTORS AFFECTING HYGROSCOPICITY

- nature and amount of colloid → increase with fineness
- adsorbed cations → depends on vapour pressure
- Temperature → decrease with increase in temp (kinetic energy ↑)

Low vapour pressure

- K, Na, NH_4 saturated soil adsorb less H_2O than H and Ca-clay
- RH of 74.9% – hygroscopicity

H > Ca > Li > Na > Ba > K.

- Ca-clay more open and absorb more H_2O than Na-clay

At high vapour pressure,

Na-saturated soil more adsorption

RH 99.8 - hygroscopicity

Li > Na > H > Ba > Ca > K.

Na-clay swells and adsorb greater than Ca-clay

HEAT OF WETTING

- wetting is an exothermic process.
- only in dry range of soils
- pF 4.5-7.0 ↳ maximum
- practically zero at hygroscopic coefficient (pF 4.5)
- Then increases as soil H_2O content decreases.
- maxm in oven dry soil.
- depends on organic matter, type of clay etc
  fineness ↑, wetting (heat) ↑.
- index of energy for adsorption of H_2O.

Rode wald's equation

$$\alpha F = E(r+i)$$

αF = Energy in attraction of H_2O to unit wt of substance

F = Surface of the wetting equivalent of heat

E = Mechanical equivn of heat

r = heat equivalent to work released by adhesion.

i = ... necessary to diminish cohesion.

$$w = \frac{Ai}{B+i}$$ | A & B are constants

↓

heat produced when 1 gm of dry soil swells up taking 1 gm of H_2O.

SOIL WATER CLASSIFICATION

→ Physical
→ Biological

Briggs (1897)

PHYSICAL

→ Hygroscopic >31 bar. (moves in vapour form)
→ Capillary
→ Gravitational

Gravitational
(between maximum retentive capacity and FC)
- influence of gravity.
- free H_2O.
- greater than (0.1 bar for coarse, 0.33 bar for fine)

Capillary
↳ continuous film around particles and capillary spaces
(1/10th bar or 1/3rd bar and 31 bar between)
Part of capillary H_2O ie upto 15 bar used by plants

BIOLOGICAL

→ Unavailable H_2O >15 bar.
→ Available H_2O (W.P – F.C) 15 bar – 0.1/0.33
4.5 – 0.1 μ diameter
→ Super available H_2O (drainage H_2O)

↓ between saturated and FC
0 bar to 0.1/0.33 bar.
- lost by drainage.
- pores > 15 μ diameter, 0 – 0.1 bar suction } drainage H_2O.
- may be harmful.

GRAVITATIONAL H_2O

Texture: sandy soil more – G. H_2O
Structure: more in granular and crumby
ESP: >15 → structureless → low G. H_2O.

CAPILLARY H_2O

Texture:– fine

OM content

↑

ESP

> 15, structureless → ↓ decreases.

HYGROSCOPIC H_2O

- finer ↑.
- expanding
- Na-saturated more because it swells more.

SOIL WATER AVAILABILITY TO PLANTS

- FC = upper limit
- PWP = lower limit.

→ Veihmeyer and Hendrickson

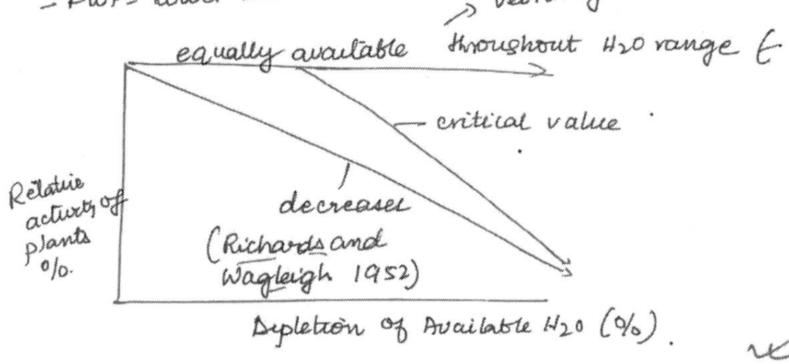

- Critical point 60-80% of available H_2O depletion.
- Main disadvantages of these hypothesis
- didn't consider climate and plant type

- concept of potential applied to soil H_2O (Buckingham, 1907)
- soil H_2O potential
  ↳ relative levels of potential energy in different locations within the soil,
  ↳ not absolute amount of potential energy
  ↓
  as pure H_2O as reference (free and pure H_2O
  ↳ in standard pressure and temperature
  in a and standard reference state
- absolute amount of potential energy—difficult to determine
- relative potential energy
  ↳ determines rate and direction of flow of H_2O.
- Therefore, soil water potential = difference between soil water potential at a specific location and that of pure water in reference state
- higher soil water potential to low soil H_2O potential.
  ↓
- due to several forces

a) gravitational forces (pull H_2O downwards)
b) adsorption and capillary forces (soil pores and particles)
c) osmotic forces (attraction of ions and solutes by H_2O)

so, — gravitational potential (ϕ_g)
matric potential (ϕ_m)
osmotic potential (ϕ_o).

d) pneumatic potential (ϕ_a) ←
↳ change in pressure of ambient air

- Another pressure potential (ϕ_p) = ma
  - In unsaturated = $\phi_m + \phi_a$
  - In saturated = due to weight of H_2O

$\phi_t = \phi_g + \phi_p + \phi_o + \ldots$

Unsaturated

$\phi_t = \phi_g + \phi_m + \phi_a + \phi_o + \ldots$

Saturated

$\phi_t = \phi_g + \phi_s + \phi_o + \ldots$

ϕ_s = submergence potential (depends on submergence depth)

$\phi_h = \phi_g + \phi_p$

↳ hydraulic potential = pressure + gravitational (p+g)

Differences between h.p at different places in the soil

↳ driving force for movement of water.

- Water potential (ϕ_w) – mao

$\phi_w = \phi_m + \phi_a + \phi_o$

directly ∝ to RH of vapour in equilm with the liquid phase in soil & plant

- measure of plant water status and in saline soil
  ↳ in osmotic potential

- Totals soil water potential

↳ amount of work that must be done ~~to~~ per unit quantity of pure H_2O in order to transport reversibly and isothermally an infinitesimal quantity of H_2O from a pool of pure water at a specified elevation at atmospheric pressure, to the soil H_2O.

~~Ter~~
- potential not measured by transporting H_2O ~~as~~
but other properties
like elevation
hydrostatic pressure
vapour pressure etc

- reversible:– no energy is lost
- isothermally:– under constant temperature
- infinitesimal ..– so that soil H_2O remains unaffected

- Main advantage

unified measure to determine state of H_2O at any time, any where within soil-plant-atm continuum.

- can be expressed on the basis of mass, volume, weight

Mass:– ergs/gm, ~~dynes~~ joules/kg → fundamental expression.

dimensions L^2/T^2 ie L^2T^{-2}

Volume: dimensions of pressure
dynes/cm^2
N/m^2
bars atm,
kilopascal, Meagapascal

~~As~~ $\frac{M}{LT^2}$ ie $ML^{-1}T^{-2}$

wt :– hydraulic head.
cm of H_2O column.

L.

- Tension and suction

  ↳ used in lieu of –ve potentials when H_2O is at sub-atmospheric pressure i.e unsaturated condition.

- Negative potentials of an unsaturated soil when expressed in terms of hydraulic head – large nos -10^5 or -10^6.
- So, to avoid it, Schofield (1935) use pF (log of –ve pressure head in cm of H_2O)

$$pF = -\log h.$$

CONVERSION FACTORS

1 dyne = 10^{-5} Newton

1 erg = 10^6 dyne.cm

1 bar = 10^6 dyne/cm² = ~~10^6 erg/gm~~

= 10^5 N/m²

= 0.9869 atm

= 100 KPa

= 100 joules/kg

= 14.50 lb/inch²

= 1020 cm of H_2O column

1 atm = 10^6 dynes/cm²

= 1.013 bar

= 1033

GRAVITATIONAL POTENTIAL (ϕ_g)

– amt of work that must be done per unit quantity of pure water in order to transport reversibly and isothermally an infinitesimal quantity of ~~soil~~ H_2O from a pool containing soln identical in composition to soil H_2O at a specified elevation of the point under consideration

- effect of vertical position
- higher the elevation, greater the ability to do work.
- strictly a field phenomenon
- independent of soil properties.
- for raising a body against gravity, work must be done and the raised body store this work in form of grav. potential energy
- work done stored per unit quantity in carrying a mass of water (m) from the reference level to point under consideration

per unit mass.

$$\phi_g = \frac{mgh}{m} = gh \quad (L^2/T^2 \text{ i.e. } L^2T^{-2})$$

per unit volume

$$\phi_g = \frac{mgh}{V} = \rho gh \quad (ML^{-1}T^{-2})$$

per unit weight

$$\phi_g = \frac{mgh}{mg} = h. \quad (L)$$

= ϕ_g above reference point = +ve
below reference point = −ve

= but the difference of ϕ_g at two diff points is always same.

PRESSURE POTENTIAL (ϕ_p) = from a pool at standard atm. pressure contains a soln ....

Tensiometer — Sub-atmosphere pressure — −ve ϕ_p

Matric potential (ϕ_m)

Reference level (water Table) — 0 ϕ_p.

Peizometer. — Super atmosphere pressure (hydrostatic pressure) — +ve ϕ_p

Submergence potential (ϕ_s)

SUBMERGENCE POTENTIAL (ϕ_s)

- Piezometer
- Hydrostatic pressure (P) = ϕ_s.
  = $\rho g h = \phi_s$.

MATRIC POTENTIAL (ϕ_m)

- interaction of soil water with soil matrix
- water in unsaturated soil → capillarity and adsorptive forces.
  ↓ produce matric potential.
  ↙ reduces energy of the pure H_2O ie less movement of H_2O

That's why work must be done to make it free.

So, matric potential = 0 or -ve.

- ϕ_m ↓ with increase in soil H_2O content
- Difference of ϕ_m in two locations - movement of H_2O
- from wet soil (higher ϕ_m) to dry soil (low ϕ_m)
- In saturation: ϕ_m = 0
  FC = ~~-10,000~~ - 1000 mm
  WC = - 15,000 mm

- Matric potential = but different sign with matric suction/tension.

So, matric suction = +ve
potential = -ve.

ISSS commission (1963) = negative gauge pressure, relative to external gas pressure on the soil H_2O, to which a soln identical in compo. with the soil soln must be subjected in order to be in equilm through a porous permeable wall with H_2O in the soil.

- Matric suction/tension - Tensiometer

PNEUMATIC POTENTIAL (ϕ_a)

- change of soil H_2O pressure due to change of gas pressure
- negligible in field (as the atm. pressure remains nearly constant)
- pressure membrane apparatus ✓

OSMOTIC POTENTIAL (ϕ_o)

- due to the presence of solutes (inorganic salts / organic / both)

solutes lower the potential

reduce free energy of H_2O → Osmosis

- So, work must be done
- There fore, always negative as matric potential
- with increase of solutes ↑, ϕ_o ↑, ↓vapour pressure. ↓ Total SWP (Soil H_2O Potential)
- not much effect in movement of H_2O in soil but in wa in soil to plants and vapour diffusion. & when semi-permeable membrane like soil-plant root interface. → only when effective barrier

$\pi = MRT$

π = Osmotic pressure dynes/cm²

M = Total molar concn of solute part (mol/m³) ↓ difficult to find

R = Universal gas constant

= 8.314×10^3 KPa m³/mol K. → 8.314 J/mol

1 cal = 4.184 J

T = Temp in °K.

per unit mass

$$\phi_o = \frac{-\pi}{\rho_w}.$$

volume

$$\phi_o = -\pi$$

atm/bar/KPa

$$\Rightarrow \phi_o = -36\, EC_e \text{ (EC of saturated)}.$$

↳ dS/m.

OVERBURDEN POTENTIAL (ϕ_Ω).

- when soil moves freely
- similar to pressure potential.
- Below H_2O table, ϕ_Ω part of submergence potential
  Above " , ϕ_Ω .. – .. matric potential
- difficult to separate

UTILITY OF SOIL H_2O POTENTIAL CONCEPT

- replaces physical classification of soil H_2O
- state of soil water – movement of H_2O

  if 0 potential = no movement

  wettest state = 0 bar

  driest state = 31 bar

  As suction → saturated soil – H_2O drawn out first from larger pores and subsequently from smaller pores.

- Unsaturated

$$\phi_t = \phi_g + \phi_m + \phi_a + \phi_o + \ldots$$

saturated

$$\phi_t = \phi_g + \phi_s + \phi_o + \ldots$$

SOIL MOISTURE CHARACTERISTIC CURVE

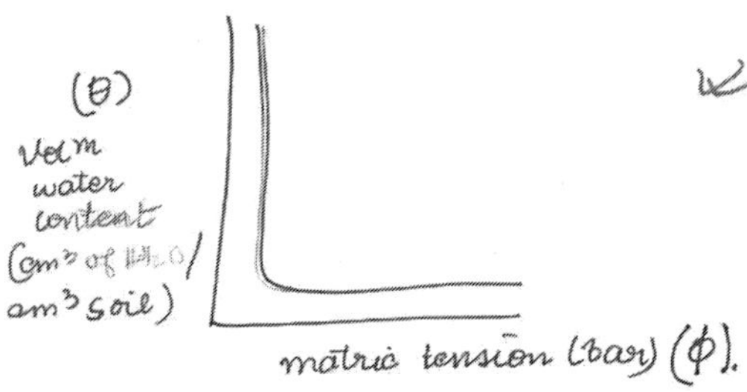

- curve showing volumetric H_2O content and matric suction
- water retention - continuous function of suction.
- ↓ decreases with increase of suction
- rapid upto 1 bar. slow upto 2 bar then after very slow
- In saturated soil, suction/tension/hydrostatic pressure = 0
- At low suction, no water released
- until a critical value known as air entry suction
- First from macropores then micropores and
- high suction, micropores and surfaces.
- Further increase of suction ⇒ ↓ thickness of hydration envelops.
- determined experimentally.
- most of H_2O held at low suction (upto 1 bar)
- From 0 to 1 bar, Low suction (high water content) water retention depends on capillarity → pore size distribution depends on → soil structure → low suction
- At higher suction (lower water content) depends on hydration envelops (adsorption) ↙ depends on soil texture & specific surface. → High suction.

- non-linear curve
  ↓
  so makes it difficult to estimate matric potentials from the measurements of vol. H_2O content & vice-versa

FACTORS AFFECTING SOIL MOISTURE CHARACTERISTIC CURVE

SOIL TEXTURE

- Water retention ↑ → clayey soil
- For a low suction, in sandy - pores emptied quickly
- So, for same volum. H_2O content, suction < in coarse textured

SOIL STRUCTURE

- important for lower suction (1 to 2 bar) upto 2 bar

- pore size distribution

CLAY MINERALS

mont > illite > kaolinite -

- montmorillonite more retention of H_2O f.b illite and kaolinite.

ORGANIC MATTER

- water retention more in organic soils //

COMPACTION

↳ reduces the porosity by decreasing macropores.

low water retention at low suction (0-1 bar)

but amount of micropores increases → so, increase H_2O retention in intermediate matric suction.

But at high matric suction – retention not affected by soil compaction → because depends on specific surface.

SOIL SOLUTION

Water retention at any matric suction is ↑ when the soln is fairly concentrated with electrolytes of divalent cations due to suppression of swelling eg Ca^{2+}.

but lower ⟶ monovalent cations such as Na^+ ↳ increase of swelling

HYSTERESIS IN SOIL MOISTURE CHARACTERISTIC CURVE

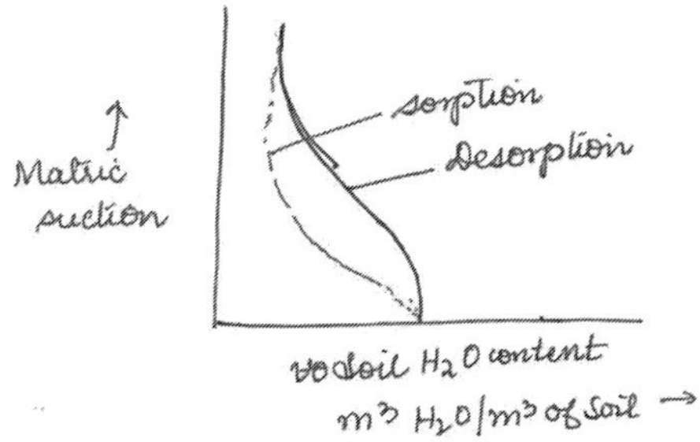

- graphs opp to SMC.

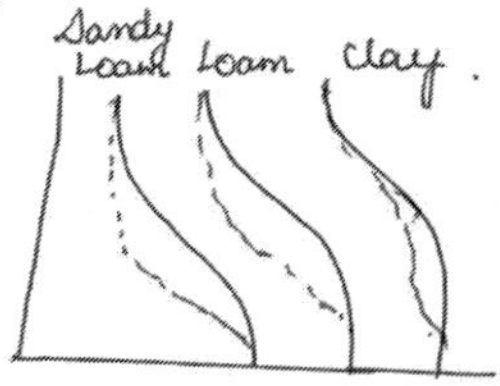

- desorption curve and sorption curve
  (drying) (wetting)
- desorption curve — gradually drying a completely saturated soil-increasing of suction to the specified matric potentials and determine vol. H_2O content
- sorption curve - gradually wetting an air dry soil to the specified matric potentials. and determine vol. H_2O content
- Both curves are continuous but not identical
- equil^m soil H_2O content at any matric suction > in desorption curve
- The relationship between soil H_2O content and ϕ_m in different curves = hysteresis.
- soil Moist. char. curves exhibit hysteresis at any stage of wetting/drying between saturation and air dryness.

CAUSES OF HYSTERESIS

- non-uniformity of pores (Ink-bottle effect) (refer Hillel)

when desorption : water will not drained until suction increased to a critical value.

adsorption : water will not enter until a suction is reduced beyond critical value.

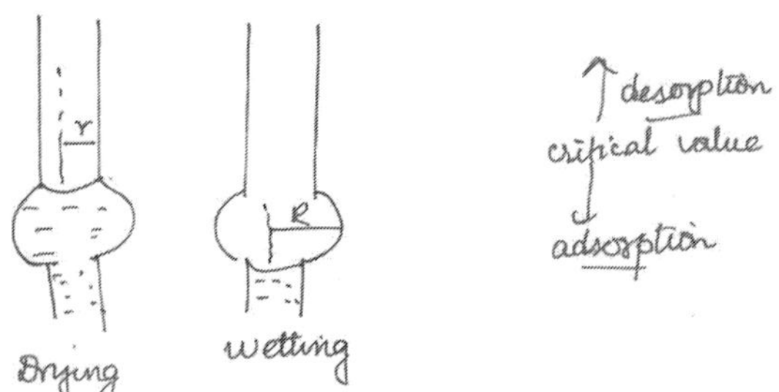

Contact angle

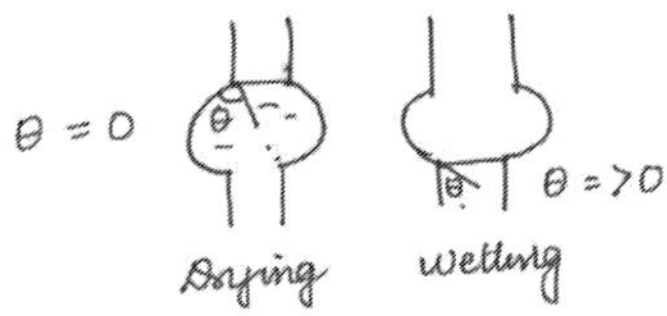

contact angle as well radius of curvature is smaller during drying.

Larger contact angle during wetting - due to presence of surface active substances and surface roughness.

- soil pore will contain more water on drying.

Entrapped air

↳ during wetting reduces penetration of H_2O in pore space

→ decrease in water content at same matric suction.

Swelling and shrinkage

- Wetting and drying — causes shrinkage and swelling ~~due~~ — results differential changes in pore space as well as pore size distribution due to change in soil structure
- may be due to internal resistance to particle rearrangement which keeps the volume higher on shrinking than on swelling.

MOVEMENT OF H_2O IN SOIL

LIQUID H_2O FLOW

- driving force- pressure gradient
- from higher potential to lower potential
  lower suction to higher suction
- saturated flow and unsaturated flow.
- Saturated flow
  no tension free water
  - in groundwater or heavy rain on surface

- when pores are completely filled with H_2O
- moving force is +ve pressure potential.

Unsaturated flow

- partly filled with H_2O, under tension.
- moving force -ve pressure gradient
  higher H_2O potential to lower potential
- water movement in soil less than saturation
  ie potential lower than -0.33 bar

WATER VAPOUR

- diffusion and mass flow
  ↓ (diffusion) due to difference in partial pressure of H_2O vapour
  ↓ (mass flow) total air pressure
- moves from moist soil atm (having high vapour pressure) to dry (low vp)
- Temp when decreases → of a moist soil
  vp ↓ → H_2O vapour moves towards the cooler part from hotter part

FUNDAMENTAL PRINCIPLES OF GROUND H_2O FLOW

LAMINAR FLOW AND TURBULENT FLOW

- Flow of liquid in tubes.
- At low velocity, inside a tube or a channel or stream - velocity is 0 at wall — due to adhesion
- In steady flow, mean flow velocity ∝ pressure drop.
- If curves are drawn for steady flow - any tangent at any point describes the direction of time average of velocity at that point - streamline

- If H_2O moving in layers, lines in which liquid particles move in time t — path line.
- When adjacent layers of water moving in parallel layers ~~lines~~ of streamline/path line in different velocities slide each other without intersection

  ↳ laminar flow.

- Osbome Reynolds (1883)
- Reynold's no (Re)

$$Re = \frac{\rho d V}{\eta}$$

ρ → density of H_2O; d → effective pore diameter; V → critical velocity (flow velocity); η → viscosity of water

- no unit
- In laminar flow.
  - in straight tubes (1000 – 2200) → turbulent flow
  - in curved tubes → Re → laminar < 1.
- If diameter of tube and flow velo. ↑ to a point where mean flow velocity not ∝ pressure drop → turbulent flow.
- turbulent eddies occur.
- Re > 1 or Re = 1.

POISEUILLE'S LAW

$$Q = \frac{V}{t} = \frac{\pi R^4 \Delta P}{8 \eta L}$$

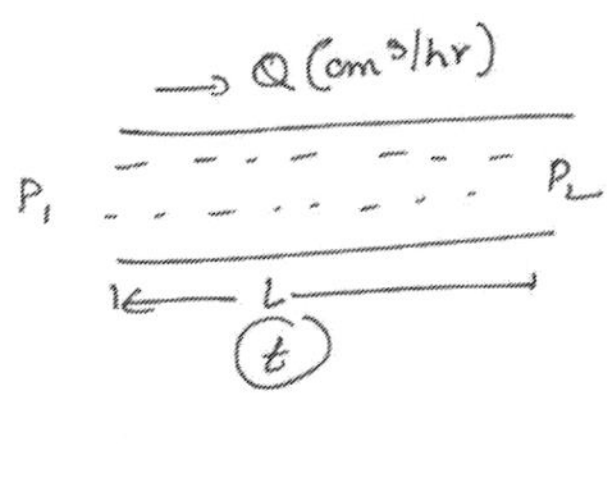

- discharge or volume flow rate Q (cm^3/hr) [being volume of H_2O flowing through a section of length (L cm) per unit time (hr)]

$\propto = \frac{\Delta P}{L}$ and R^4.

↳ pressure drop per unit length.

$$Q = \frac{V}{t}$$

$$\frac{Q}{At} = \frac{cm^3}{cm^2/min} \Rightarrow cm/min = q \text{ (flux)}$$

$$\boxed{Q = \frac{\pi R^4 \Delta P}{8\eta L}}$$

$$Q = \frac{\pi R^2 R^2 \Delta P}{8\eta L}$$

q = flux
= cm/hr $= \frac{Q}{A} = \frac{Q}{\pi R^2}$

$$\Rightarrow \frac{Q}{\pi R^2} = \frac{R^2 \Delta P}{8\eta L}$$

$$\Rightarrow \boxed{q = \frac{R^2}{8\eta} \frac{\Delta P}{L}}$$

Assumption
- flow is steady or streamline
- constant pressure along cross sect
- uniform radius

So, flux or flow rate per unit area $\propto R^2$ (of pores)

η = dynes-sec/cm²
= poise.

P_1 = dynes/cm²

P_2 = dynes/cm²

→ use in determining hydraulic conductivity

DARCY'S LAW

- French engineer Henry Darcy (1856)
- flow of H_2O through a column of sand filtered beds.
- volume flow rate Q (cm³/hr) $\propto$ cross-sectional area and hydraulic head drop and $\propto 1/\alpha$ to the length of the soil column.

Hydraulic head drop.

$$Q = \frac{V}{t} = \frac{A \Delta H}{L}$$

$\frac{\Delta H}{L}$ — hydraulic gradient (i)

(driving force of H_2O flow through a porous medium

↳ dimensionless

$Q = \frac{V}{t}$

$\Rightarrow \frac{Q}{A} = \frac{V}{At} \Rightarrow \frac{V}{At} = \frac{A \Delta H}{LA}$

$\Rightarrow q = \frac{V}{At}$

$\Rightarrow \frac{V}{At}$

~~$\Rightarrow q = \frac{\Delta H}{L}$~~

So, $q \propto i$

$q = Ki$

Assumption

- Laminar flow
- $Re < 1$
- porous medium
- no attraction betwn fluid & medium
- Isothermal
- fluid be incompressible ↓ like H_2O not like honey

$\Rightarrow q = K \frac{\Delta H}{L}$

↳ proportionality constant ↓ known as hydraulic conductivity which relates flux with the driving force.

- In terms of water potential ϕ

$q = K \frac{\Delta \phi}{L}$

indicates property of the conducting medium to transmit H_2O

Dimension of HC same as flux = LT^{-1}

= cm/sec.

LIMITATIONS OF DARCY's LAW

- Only under saturated situation – low flow velocities as long as hydraulic gradient and flux ratio is linear.
- upto laminar flow i.e. $Re < 1$.

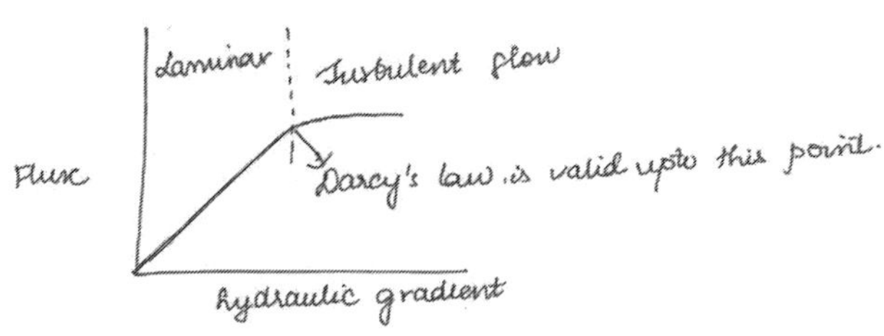

$Re = 1–10$

- So, only in heavy soil ✓
- when pore size increases (in sandy) → turbulent → Darcy's Law fail

- also can also occur in heavy soil

↓

when no flow or only low flow rates less than proportional to the hydraulic gradient

↓

at very low hydraulic gradients

- Reason for deviation:–

at low gradient – H_2O more rigid than bulk water

↓

due to close proximity with soil part and strong adsorptive forces

↓

exhibits properties of Bingham liquid (low yield value)

than Newtonian fluid.

↓

develop structure like ice.

- Threshold gradient: by extrapolating the linear relations.

↓

Below → flux = 0 or flux is lower than predicted by Darcy's equation

Beyond — flux is prop to hydraulic gradient.

EQUATION FOR SATURATED FLOW

Darcy's equation – saturated water flow – under steady state – in homogeneous and isotropic porous media

$$q = -K\nabla H \quad \text{(three dimension)}$$

q ↓ flux $= \frac{Q}{A}$

K ↓ saturated hydraulic conductivity

∇H ↓ hydraulic gradient

K = scalar

∇H = vector

q = vector

= direction of flow determined by ∇H

= -ve sign:- H_2O flow opp to hydraulic gradient

= Darcy's law ~ saturated condition

↓

flow of H_2O through a homog. & isotropic porous medium $\propto$ to the driving force ~~and~~ in direction of flow and $\propto$ ~~of~~ conductivity

$$q_x = -K \frac{dH}{dx}$$

$q_x \rightarrow$ flux in x direction

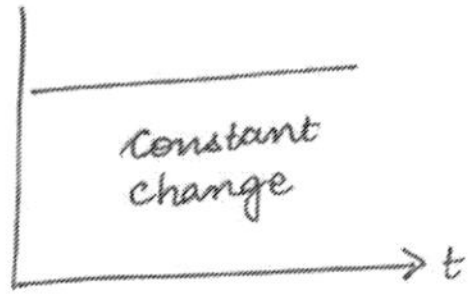

steady flow

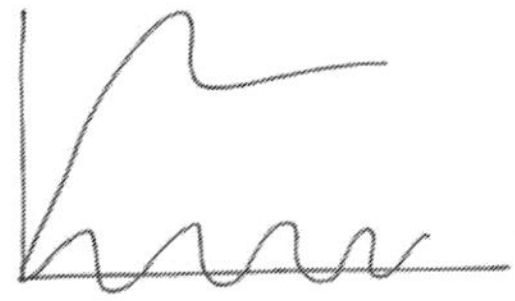

transient flow.

- ~~In~~ But in unsteady or transient flow → magnitude and direction of flux and potential gradient vary.

↓

so, introduction of law of conservation of matter essential.

↓

expressed in form of ~~law of~~ eq^n of continuity

If rate of inflow > rate of outflow – vol^m of soil gain excess H_2O → ↑ in H_2O storage.

rate inflow < rate of outflow – soil loosing stored H_2O ↓ in H_2O storage.

$$\frac{\partial \theta}{\partial t} = -\frac{\partial q_x}{\partial x}$$ — rate of increase of flux q_x with x

↙ rate of decrease of vol H_2O content with time.

= Multidimensions

$$\frac{\partial \theta}{\partial t} = -\nabla q$$

$$\Rightarrow \frac{\partial \theta}{\partial t} = -\nabla q_x$$

$$\Rightarrow \frac{\partial \theta}{\partial t} = -\nabla(-K\nabla H)$$

$$= \nabla K \nabla H.$$

In one dimensional

$$\frac{\partial \theta}{\partial t} = \frac{\partial}{\partial x}\left(K \frac{\partial H}{\partial x}\right)$$

<u>Assumptions</u>

- inertial forces negligible ✓
- H_2O continuously flowing ✓
- isothermal condition ✓
- fluid/porous medium not changed by chemical/biological process.

If soil saturated, $\frac{\partial \theta}{\partial t} = 0$

So. $K_S \frac{\partial^2 H}{\partial x^2} = 0$

K_s = HC of saturated soil.

$$\frac{\partial^2 H}{\partial x^2} + \frac{\partial^2 H}{\partial y^2} + \frac{\partial^2 H}{\partial z^2} = 0. \rightarrow \text{Laplace equation}$$

↓

2nd order partial differential eq^n.

$$\nabla H = 0$$

<u>Uses</u>

- to obtain a quantitative description of H_2O flow by specifying <u>boundary</u> conditions.

TERMINOLOGY

HYDRAULIC HEAD

- numerical equivalent of the ht. of H_2O column excerting a force equal to attractive force betw soil & H_2O.
- elevation with respect to standard datum at which H_2O stands in a riser pipe. connected to a point in question in soil.
- includes elevation (gravitational head), pressure head and velocity head.
- For laminar flow, velocity head negligible.
- Units : cm, m
- common name of total potential head.
- potential function ie p.e per unit wt of soil H_2O.
- known as hydraulic potential
- driving force for steady state liquid flow under isothermal condition.
- solute potential – imp only when there is semi-permeable membrane – so, not imp in soil.

so. hydraulic head/potential = total soil potential – solute poten.

= gravitational head determined by vertical distance of point from reference

= pressure head = ht of H_2O column resting on that pt.

$H_t = H_g + H_p$

$H_g = \rho g z$ — ρ = density of H_2O gm/cm³; z = distance of A from ref. (in cm); g = accn due to gr. cm/sec²

= dynes/cm²

$H_p = \rho g h$ → distance from free H_2O surface in cm.

$$H_t = \rho g z + \rho g h$$
$$= \rho g (z + h)$$
$$= H \rho g \quad (H = z + h)$$

- Measurements
  - saturated soil (piezometer)
  - unsaturated (tensiometer)

HYDRAULIC GRADIENT

$= \frac{\Delta H}{L}$

= Total head prodrop per unit distance in the direction of flow.

= no dimension.

$\Delta H = H_1 - H_2$ → at outflow boundary

↓

hy. heads at inflow boundary

TORTUOSITY

- average ratio of $\frac{\text{actual length of flow path of liquid}}{\text{straight length}}$.

Tortuosity $= \frac{L_e}{L}$ — actual distance

T always > 1 and may exceed 2.

- no dimension.
- can be measured from determ.-of electrical resistivity Es of soil in saturated condition. with a liquid of known resistivity.

$$\frac{L_e}{L} = \sqrt{\frac{\varepsilon E_s}{E}}$$

ε ⇒ porosity or area of conducting channel/unit area of cross section.

FLUX AND FLUX VELOCITY

↳ rate of flow

quantity of material/energy transferred through a system of in unit time.

- mass flux
- volume flux
- heat flux
- flux density = flux per unit area
  ↳ quantity of H_2O transported per unit area in unit time

$$q = \frac{V}{At}$$

dimension $= LT^{-1}$

⇒ flux = flux velocity (in pipe)

But in soil,

flux < flux velocity.

Reasons:-

- flow doesn't take place through entire cross-sec. area of soil – soil particles reduce this area.
- actual length of path in soil greater than length of soil column.

PERMEABILITY

- ease with which a porous medium transmits H_2O/air.
- qualitative sense
- properties of fluid
- dimension LT^{-1}
  cm/sec.

INTRINSIC PERMEABILITY (K')

- Rate of flow dependent on soil char. only. → total porosity, distribution of pore sizes & tortuosity.

- Hc depends on both soil prop & fluid prop.
- But k' – only on soil properties.

$K = k'f \rightarrow$ fluidity $\frac{1}{LT} = \frac{1}{cm.sec}$

- dimension of (L^2) ie
ie cm^2

- k' = very small → practically μ^2 (square micron)

- Hc (K) → different for all fluids
K + same for a stable soil.

FLUIDITY

- fluid properties that control rate of flow
↳ viscosity and density

- $K = k'f$

$f = \frac{\rho g}{\eta}$ ($L^{-1}T^{-1}$)

$\Rightarrow K = k' \frac{\rho g}{\eta}$

⇒ change in fluidity = Temp & electrolyte concn.
↑ → ↓ viscosity
↓
↑ fluidity
↓
↑ HC(K).

HYDRAULIC CONDUCTIVITY

HC of a saturated condition = permeability

- HC being slope of linear relation between flux & r

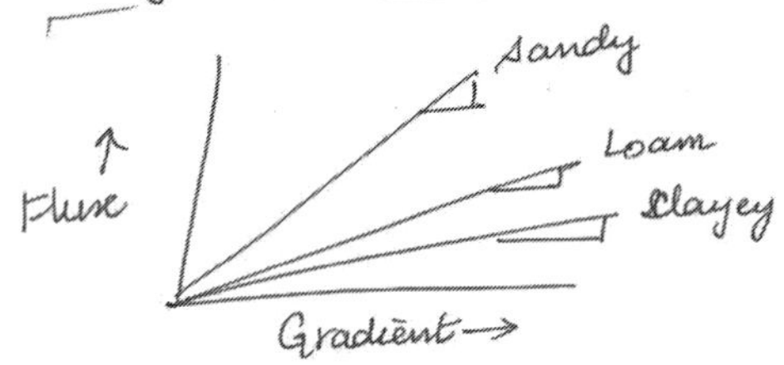

FACTORS AFFECTING PERMEABILITY OR HC OF A SATURATED SOIL

→ As K = K'f

HC depends on intrinsic permeability and fluidity

and ↓ depends on porosity → on macropores ↓ depends on soil texture, soil aggregation etc.

Soil texture

saturated K is high in (maxm) sandy soils and it decrease with decrease in coarseness.

- Texture finer than sandy clay loam may not follow this — because, in fine textured soils, soil aggre. may overide the effect of soil texture

Soil structure

- maxm in spheroidal type
  minm in plate like
- more aggregation — more non-capillary pores - more HC.

Compaction

- decreases non capillary pores / total porosity
- reduces K.

Exchangeable cations

- Na → dispersion — slow permeability — low K.
- Ca → better → higher K.

- Orga...

- improves K.
(formation of water stable aggregates)

Fluidity
↳ depends on concn and comp of salts dissolved in H_2O and viscosity
↳ depends on temp, electrolyte concn of salt → low
salt → NaOH or Na_2CO_3 → dispersion → ↓K.

As temp ↑, viscosity ↓. → K ↑.

HC → standardized at 20°C and temperature correction: –

$$K_{20} = K_T \frac{\eta_T}{\eta_{20}}$$

FLOW OF H_2O IN UNSATURATED

- Most of agricultural soils.
- soil H_2O potentials are lower than –0.33 bar (more –ve)
- Rate of flow increases with ↑ in H_2O potential and size of pores.

- Flow of H_2O more complicated
↳ difficult to describe quantitatively

because state and content of H_2O is changed during the flow involving complex relations.

DIFFERENCE BETWEEN SATURATED AND UNSATURATED SOILS

- Saturated : pores filled with H_2O, no tension

(i) Unsaturated : macropores – air
micropores – water , under tension.

(Both cases, H_2O flows from higher pot. gradient to lower)

- Moving force in
Sat : +ve pressure potential (gravit. potential is disregarded)

(ii) H_2O flows from higher hydrostatic pressure to lower hydrostatic pressure

unsaturat : –ve pressure potential termed as suction / tension
H_2O flows from zone of lower matric suction to higher matric suction eg. –1 atm to –10 atm

- at saturation, most conductive soil – with macropores

(iii) so, sandy soil - conducts H_2O more rapidly

- at unsaturated, reverse
so, clayey soil, conducts H_2O more rapidly

- In aggregated soils, the interaggregate spaces – macropores in unsaturated condition :– H_2O remains in the capillary wedges at the contact point of the particles.

(iv) So, in saturation – macropores – high flow of water
in unsaturation – macropores - barrier to water flow
↓ decrease in movement of H_2O in unsaturation

- Darcy's Law – flux ∝ potential gradient

(v) slope of flux and gradient → hydraulic conductivity

In saturated flow, HC → independent of magnitude of H_2O potential

unsaturated → HC → values vary with suction
HC decrease with ↑ in suction.

(VI) – actual flow path in unsaturated longer in unsaturated soil → increase in tortuosity &

so, movement of H_2O in unsaturated → less than saturated soil → because

Darcy's law states flux $\propto \frac{1}{}$ length of flow path.

– unsaturated :– macropores filled with air
↳ reduces cross-sectional area available for flow → ↓ K → so. (VI*)

– In unsaturation: suction develops.

Poiseuille's law → volume flow rate $\propto r^4$

flux $\propto r^2$

so, K $\propto r^2$ of pores.

so, if size of pores ↓ 1/3 rd →

volume flow rate $\propto \left(\frac{1}{3}\right)^4$

$= \frac{1}{81}$ th.

flux $= 1/9$ th.

– For all these reasons, soil H_2O content decreases from saturation → steep drop in K → drop 10^6 times sometimes

K IN UNSATURATED SOIL

– flux (q) = not linearly related with hydraulic gradient
↳ so, Darcy's equation becomes non-linear

so, K depends on θ (vol. H_2O content)
ψ (suction)

- If flux vs suction/moisture gradient a fixed ψ/θ, straight line.

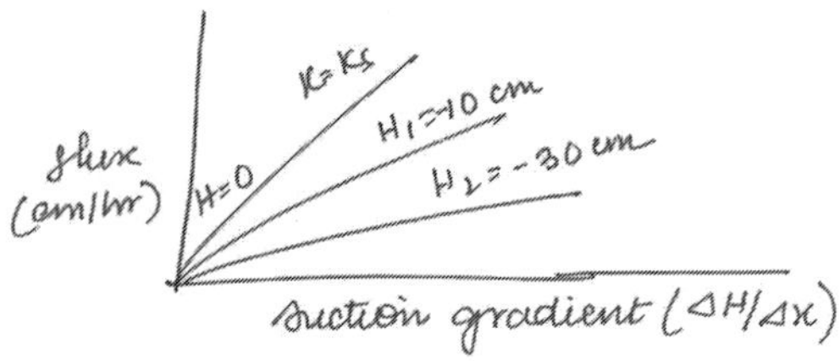

slope of each line = K..

- K of unsaturated soil ↓ with ↓ in water content or ↑ in suction
- So, darcy's law modified with provision that K is a function of ψ (suction head) or (vol. water content) θ

So, $K = K(\psi)$

$K = K(\theta)$

So, $q = -K(\psi)\nabla H$ — includes both pressure head (h) or suction head (ψ) and gravitational head (z) $(h + z + \psi)$

$q = -K(\theta)\nabla H$

↳ affected by hysteresis more than $K(\theta)$

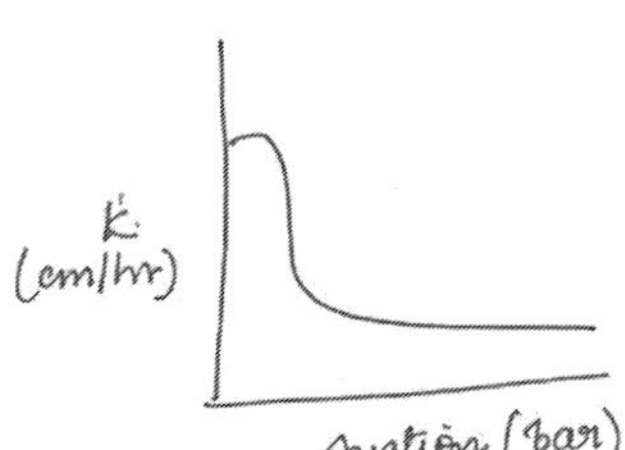

$K = K(\psi)$

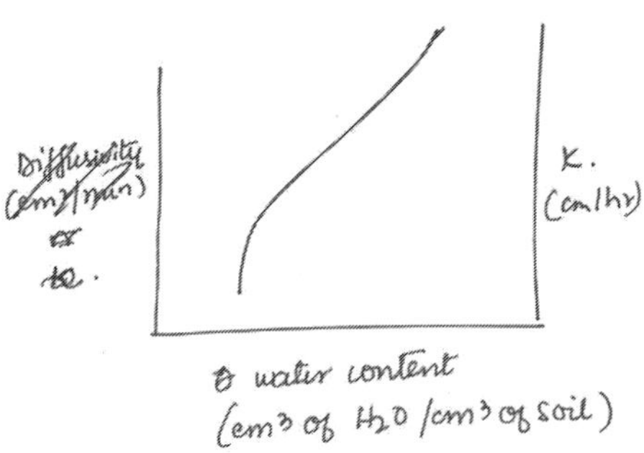

$K = K(\theta)$

- HC in coarse textured soil becomes lower than fine textured.

Reason

moving force : suction gradient

As suction increases → ↓ soil H_2O content → ↓ HC

- Gardner (1960) — eq^n between K and suction/θ

HC at any vol. H_2O content ← $K = \frac{a}{\psi^m}$

$$K = \frac{a}{b + \psi^m}$$

$$K = \frac{K_S}{1 + (\psi/\psi_c)^m}$$ — K_S — HC at saturation

$$K = a\theta^m$$

$$K = K_S S^m$$

a, b, m = constants

ψ = matric suction

θ = vol. H_2O content

S = degree of saturation

ψ_c = suction head at which $K = \frac{1}{2} K_S$.

FACTORS AFFECTING HYDRAULIC CONDUCTIVITY IN UNSATURATED SOILS

→ soil H_2O content

→ nature of the soil

Nature of the soil

- More micropores, more K.
- So, fine textured, more K.

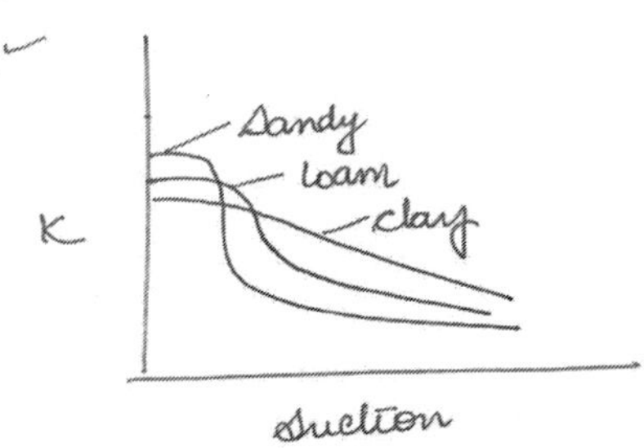

So, K = sand < loam < clay

- K of aggregates decreases rapidly — as size of agg. ↑.
  with ↓ water content (moist range)
- So, well aggregated surface soil layer — soil H_2O conservation
- In dry range, K → no effect due to Structure
  depends on texture
- Soil compaction → reduce macropores
  But ↑ micropores — so ↑ K.
  But continuous and heavy compaction → ↓ K.
- Sodicity — dispersion → ↓ K both sat & unsat.

SOIL H_2O CONTENT

K ↓ with decrease in soil water content

Reasons

↓ effective porosity, pore conductivity (Poiseuille's law $Q \propto r^4$)
for withdrawal of H_2O from large pores.

↑ in tortuosity

↓ size of pores.

EQUATION OF H_2O FLOW IN UNSAT. SOIL

$$q = -K(\psi)\,\nabla H$$
$$q = -K(\theta)\,\nabla H$$

DIFFUSIVITY

- simpler mathematical form of H_2O flow and
- easy to estimate experimentally
- less affected by hysteresis.

Assumption

flux of water ∝ water content gradient.

$$-\frac{\partial\theta}{\partial\psi} = C(\theta) \qquad \theta \cdot \frac{\partial\theta}{\partial\psi}$$

↳ specific water capacity

= slope of SMCC at any particular value of θ

⇒ Soil water diffusivity $D(\theta) = \frac{K(\theta)}{C(\theta)}$ — $K(\theta)$: unsaturated hydraulic conductivity; $C(\theta)$: specific water capacity

- dimension — L^2T^{-1} (L^2T^{-1})

  $cm^2\,sec^{-1}$

- Advantages
- range of values is narrow – easy to draw in graph paper
- less affected by hysteresis

Disadvantage

- must know the values of $K(\theta)$ and $C(\theta)$ But very small values so, difficult to calculate diffusivity

$$\frac{\partial\theta}{\partial t} = \frac{\partial}{\partial x}\left[D(\theta) \cdot \frac{\partial\theta}{\partial x}\right]$$

↳ analagous to Fick's diffusion equation

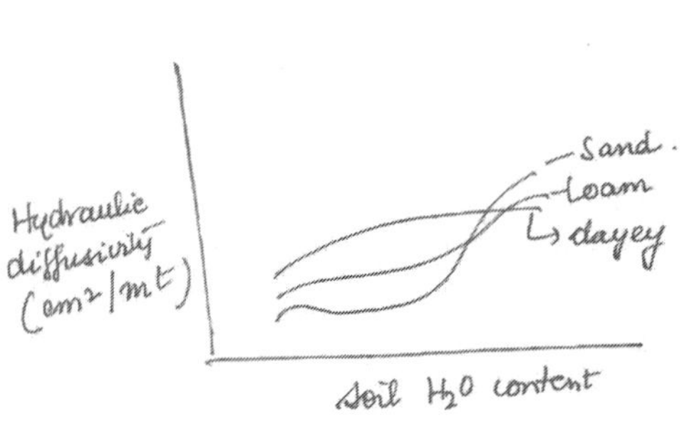

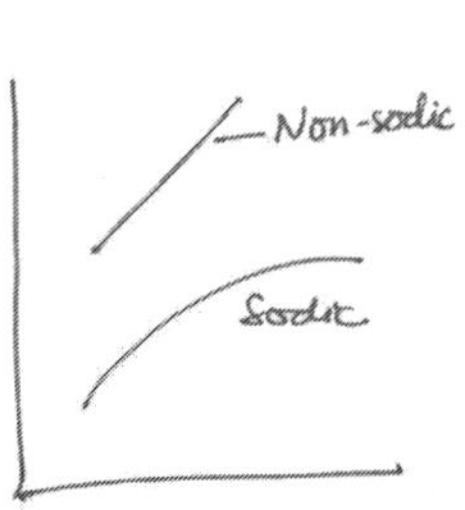

- ~~ct~~ $D(\theta)\uparrow$ with increase in soil H_2O content

$D(\theta)$ = ~~ae+~~ $ae^{b\theta}$

a, b } constants
e = exponential

- Sometimes, in dry soils $D(\theta)\uparrow$ with ↓ in θ due to movement of water vapour.

In wet soil → $D(\theta)\to\infty$ (infinity) as ~~C~~$(\theta)\to 0$ and so, ~~dt~~ $D(\theta)$ can't be determined as soil water con is at or near saturation
tends

- $D(\theta)\to$ like unsaturated K → influenced by soil texture, soil structure, compaction, sodicity and soil H_2O content (same effect)

Equation of capillarity

$$P_i - P_a = \Delta P = \gamma\left(\frac{1}{R_1}+\frac{1}{R_2}\right)$$

pressure of soil water, can be smaller than atmospheric

P_a = atmospheric pressure. conventionally taken as zero

ΔP = pressure deficit

γ = surface tension of water

R_1, R_2 = principal radii of curvature of a point on the meniscus, taken as negative when the meniscus is concave.

SOIL COLOUR

- Lithochromic colour
  (from parent material)
- Genetic or acquired colour
  (soil forming process)
- Light however is invisible itself.
- ~~w~~ Colours — Wavelength (μ) (PBG YOR)

Colours	Wavelength (μ)
Purple	0.38 – 0.45
Blue	0.45 – 0.49
Green	0.49 – 0.57
Yellow	0.57 – 0.60
Orange	0.60 – 0.62
Red	0.62 – ~~0~~.75

- colour depends on the wavelength of light it reflects or emits.
- By means of spectroreflectometer
  ↓
  contribution of various wavelengths to the total light reflected from soil.

~~CAU~~ CAUSES OF SOIL COLOUR

- minerals coatings.
- hydration
- Reduced Fe – bluish green
- mottling – due to solubilization of soil minerals eg. Fe, Mn. – during alternate wetting and drying.
- oxidation and reduction
- Moist soil – more darker
  - more absorption of light
  - more penetration
  - less reflected.

DETERMINATION OF SOIL COLOUR

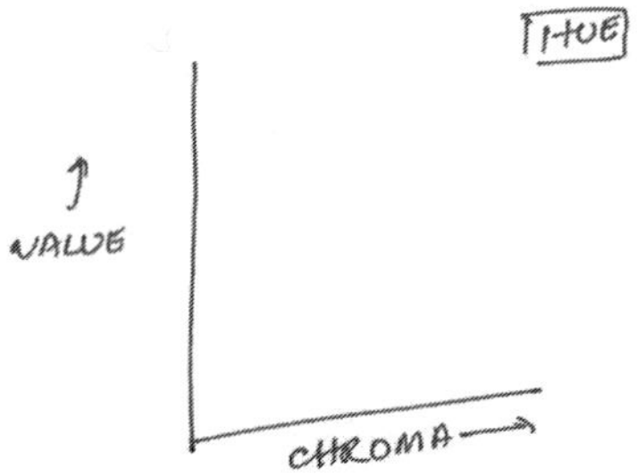

- most common
  199 diff. coloured chips
- Munsell colour charts
- ~~hue~~ hue, value and chroma

- hue - dominant spectral (rainbow) colour
  - dominant wavelength of light
  ↳ 0 to 10 → as no. ↑ — more yellow and less red.
  10R to 5Y. hue ranges in soil.
- Middle — 5 → zero point coincides with ~~the~~ 10 point of next redder hue
  5YR → middle of yellow-red hue extending from 10R (0 YR) to 10YR (zero Y).

- Value - degree of lightness and darkness in relation to a neutral scale.
  ↳ approx. √ of the total amount of light
- 0 - 10 — pure white. eg. 5/ or 0/
  ↓
  pure black
- Grey half way

- Chroma - relative purity or strength of spectral colour.
  - ↑ with decreasing ↓ greyness.
  - 0 to 8
    ↓ ↘ strongest
    neutral

- achromatic colours (pure grey, white & black) - ~~0 chroma, hue,~~ value
  0 chroma, 0 hue
  value N2/ to N8/.

3 -- Soil H_2O
4 — Soil texture, structure, hydration
5 — Volume & Mass relationship, soil colour.
6 — Remote Sensing.
7 — soil air, temp

Soil Physics

8 — chemical composition of Soil
9 — Soil alkalinity & acidity
10 — Soil colloids & Ion absorption

Soil Chemistry

11 —
12
13
14 —
15
16
17

Biology

Soil ~~Fertility~~

18
19
20
21
22

fertility

Soil Biology

23
24
25
26

Soil Pedology

27
28
29
30

Statistics